With the collaboration of
Michael Deh

Special thanks to everyone who collaborated in the making of this book.

Copyright 2013. Sebastien Dehi

All rights reserved. No part of this book may be reproduced or transmitted in any form or by any means, electronic or mechanical, including photocopying, recording, or by any information storage and retrieval system, without permission in writing from the publisher.

Printed in the United States of America

ISBN-13: 978-0615915043

Prologue

This book is not an autobiography. It is the fruit of inspiration by one's life. Strange similarities of events in both our lives compelled me to write this book over a decade ago.

Being from two separate regions of the African continent with no apparent tie, except we happen to share the same last name with an *"i"* as the only difference: Michael *Deh*. Sebastien *Dehi*.

As the conversation progresses, I learned that Michael's grandma was making pancakes to raise him; which inspired the title of this book *THE PANCAKE BOY*. My mother was making pancakes on another side of the continent to take care of us and send us to school, which led me to be able to write these lines. Education was not granted there back then and not all the parents were willing to send their kids to school. But that's another story.

Michael was born in Canada and shipped to Africa as a diplomatic package for survival… I was born in Africa and motivated by my mother to immigrate to Canada for survival.

As our journeys evolve, we all end up in the city of Toronto, and there, out of millions of people living in Canada, we end up having a common friend, whose place we met that summer of 1998.

It was there and then that Michael opened up and shared his childhood struggle, his fight for survival, our common fight for survival in a crowd where we still feel alone because we're from different parts of the world...but deep down, we all share the same story that will never be known, until told.

Thank you, Michael Deh, for sharing your story.

Sincerely,

Sebastien Dehi

The Letter

It's four o'clock. Bright sky. Rush hour. There is a huge congestion on Yonge Street as usual. Angry drivers incessantly blow car horns, snarls on their faces, mouths mouthing *f-words*. It is a typical afternoon in downtown Toronto.

Michael, biracial, 6'2", mid-thirties, athletic stature, backpack on, rides easily on the back of his race bicycle. Suddenly, he starts to speed through the rows of cars. Sweat streaming from every pore of his face. He is tired, breathless, yet he doesn't stop, especially not now; he mustn't lose even a second. Every bit of time counts. He can't allow time to escape again. To stop it would be the ultimate solution. Yes! If he could just stop time and start a new countdown, a new beginning. For everything... Everything, but *him*. *He* is unstoppable... Yes! All except the time... this damn routine in which destiny had defined his faith.

Every day, every night, even today, at this very moment, he asks himself the same question, "Why me?" Still no answer. He tries to distance himself, either flee or chase it away, but like a relentless predator determined to capture its prey, it only comes charging back, even more fiercely and powerful, unrelenting, insatiable, challenging, *"Hey, Michael! I'm still here. You can't escape. I'm a part of you and you are a piece of me. We are bound together, for better or worse."*

"No! This has to stop," Michael whispers hoarsely to himself. Enough is enough. He must get to his chosen emissary quickly. This man is his last hope, his only chance. So he is convinced. Tired or not, he has to reach him, before it is too late. As the words pound agonizingly in his head, he pedals, steadily pedals and pedals, and pedals.

Michael pedals with determination strong enough to break the chain of his bike. Yes! This is it! To break the chain is what it would take indeed....What he has to do is to break the chain of events now or he will never have peace of mind and forget the burden of dredging up the past. Forget the fairytale endings, the aftermath of help that always comes too late. Of course, he would cheer at the appointed moment: Who hasn't after such effort? Victory is always sweet after hard work... But Michael does not want to contemplate this right now; he does not even care about the aftermath. The inevitable always happens, no matter what precautions we take, anyway. It's a matter of principle, the ultimate law of retroactivity. "The price of sin", his Grandma would have said. Ah, Grandma! She has a lot to do with the final cut; but the one who really created the mess is the one he sought after now. If he brought him up the way he did, he must certainly know why. He, Michael only follows the path destiny has drawn for him. Of course, he could not forget what his Grandma said to him one day when he kept asking her: "Why do things happen to some people the way they do?" Her answer was very simple: "If you sow your seed, you must be ready to harvest its fruit." But did he plant any seed? He asked himself. Not really, except he was the fruit of one seed. He smiled. A thousand light bulbs illuminate his mind. He just got it. Of *course*, nobody else *but* him could understand the thoughts that cross his mind right now. One thing was sure: He got it. No more self-pity. Not anymore!

Michael takes a deep breath, reassures himself, but still he won't slow down; playing the blame game helps nobody at this point. Still, he is sure that his parents must be held accountable for everything; especially his father-he is the one mostly responsible. He's the one who kept his mouth shut. All those years he never dared utter the smallest word in Michael's defense, not even to say, "Enough! Michael is also my child; he is not good-for-nothing. He has his dreams and aspirations, just like any other child... Michael, don't listen to them, I'm on your side, son."

His whole life, that's all Michael needed: words, just words, even if his father did not mean them. Simply talk to him, like a father to a son. But for him, as long as his nice little family is intact from the outside, life goes on. What about him, Michael, the first born of the family? Was it asking too much of a father? Not really! He just didn't want to waste his breath on an interfering intruder like him. *"An intruder? Me?"* Michael shakes his head. He didn't want to rock the boat again. He had his own way to deal with all that: Bury his emotions deep down, stay distant and hoping one day, it would all go away. Not anymore! The time had come for a reckoning.

He slows down, stretches his hand around to touch his backpack and smiles. The package is safe. He straightens up, builds up speed, and holds on tightly to the handlebars as he dives downhill on Yonge Street among endless rows of cars. No complacence, this package has to reach its final destination. It has to land in his father's hands. And he must read it. Whether on his deathbed or not, he finally has to face all the pain and hurt that Michael, suffered as a boy and continues to live with now. His father's Leukemia has always been his lifelong rival, though certainly not the cause of this bitterness, this pain that still afflicts him as a man. His father must know what he has done to him before leaving this world. At the same time, Michael doesn't want him to use his last bit of energy or take his final breath afterwards, due to this complicated matter. He really doesn't want it, but if that is what it takes, so be it. He just wants him to know of the pain he has caused him as a child and how it made his life unbearable. In the past, in the present, and, who knows for how long? His father must know it. He must answer for himself. He must read the letter. He will understand maybe how he ruined his life.

Michael breaks hard at this last thought, holds very still, slowly wipes his forehead, and shakes his head at the idea of his parents ruining his life. *"What am I saying?"* He murmurs to himself. *"My own parents ruined my life? Of course not. How ungrateful of a son! What parents would intentionally try to ruin the lives of their own kids? They wish for them to enjoy nothing but the best in life. Sometimes things are just what they were meant to be and nothing could change their course. The same we will say of the essence of our being...That everything we are or become is set for us since our mother's embryo"*. Michael's mind went on and on to finally recollect one of his Grandma's favorite quotes: "Progression within the family is only a stage; a necessary and fated stage. All the rest lies in our hands to turn the forest into a dwelling place." It was kind of hard in his child's mind to process that thought, but now he got it.

Michael takes another deep breath. Calmer…Temporarily at peace with himself, he starts all over, his race against the clock, with a cynical smile on his face. He wants to revisit the early stage of his life with its sporadic good times, to reshape it in the form of a happy future, from a different angle. Why not? But before that, his father must be made to answer for his actions, laid out before him, the rejected one. Repentance is certainly not one of his strong virtues – a family trait- but this time there is no other way around it. His father will have to make an effort and atone.

Pedaling hard for the last half-hour, one would think that some supernatural strength had taken over him. Athletic? He has always been. He is proud of his physical ability; it made him the person that he is now: Against all odds. Most certainly, he doesn't regret his career choice, absolutely not! Soon, he will compete in the National section for the Olympic Games in Tae-

Kwon Do. His long life dream requires that both body and mind be absolutely fit. The temporary pain on a small bicycle is insignificant compared to the torment he feels deep down in his heart and stomach. And that is what needs to heal. Now! That's why this letter must reach his father as soon as possible.

More than ever before, Michael felt the strength, the eagerness to go ahead with this. He dodges in and out of traffic, up and down the hills, between cars, undaunted. The drivers blast their horns and yell at him. Michael rides by, smiles, totally disregards them – everything but not at the expense of jeopardizing his own life. He knows better. The letter has to be in his father's hands within the next few days. His countryman's visit to the motherland gives him an extraordinary opportunity that he can't miss.

It's five o'clock. Michael parks in front of a three-story apartment block in a rundown section of town. The gate to the main entrance is locked. "*Unusual!*" Michael bangs on the door loudly. A few minutes later, a middle-aged man African immigrant, clean head and chubby, comes down the stairs. It's Sheck. His face wears a mixed expression of wonder on his face, when he sees Michael. He does a double take from head to toe,

"What's up, Mike? You look as though someone just put a hose on you."

"I know… but the letter. It's important that you give this letter to my father as soon as you get there. Put it in your bag and make sure you don't lose it. Otherwise, I'm finished."

"What's up with this mysterious letter, Champ?"

"I'm not a champion! And don't keep calling me Champ. I told you that."

"Of course you are!"

"You know Sheck, you and others may see me as a champion but I don't." He looks at the letter. "This is my only chance. This could be the only thing that will help me become a true champion as you believe."

"What's wrong, Michael? I've never seen you this upset." Sheck gestures towards the open door. "Come on up with me. I still have two hours, you can tell me everything."

Michael follows. Once in the apartment, he sits down. Sheck gives him a glass of ice-cold water. He hesitates for a brief moment, and then downs the whole glass in one long mouthful.

"You know Sheck, as unbelievable as it may sound to you; my life is a true nightmare."

"I don't believe you, Michael. I mean… you're the one always in control of everything… With your strength of character, with the position you hold in society... I mean, you own your own business! I can't believe that you, Michael, are bringing yourself down because of some small, unknown problem!"

"You all say the same thing. But as a matter-of-fact, it's not just a small problem. You may find this hard to believe, but I'm hurting. I really am. It's a long story and it'd take too long to explain."

"Talk to me! Tell me everything. I have all the time in the world."

Sheck settles comfortably into his armchair, waiting for Michael to talk.

"My father has to have this letter as soon as possible. I want you to give it to him as soon as you get there. He's at the University Medical Center. It's next to the airport… the high school days…" Sheck's face lights up. "Oh yes! The prime days of The P… " Sheck swallows the words as Michael rises, contorts his face in defiance towards him. No name calling right now. Michael does not want to hear it. Sheck gets it. He stepped back, hands in the air. "Your letter will be the first thing I unpack, I promise"

Sheck pauses for a moment then continues somewhat more seriously. "Really, what's worrying you so much?"

Michael opens his mouth but closes it again. He doesn't know where to begin. He can't come up with the words to express how much pain he feels. The words he thought of were too light. They would only distort the truth. He has been keeping his pain inside since childhood, never daring to tell anyone. He always knew how to keep it a secret and this wasn't the moment to betray his inner voice. No! Not a single word. Sheck insists but Michael shakes his head, quickly reaffirming his intention to say not one word. It is only to his father and to him exclusively, that he will direct those words best exchanged between individuals of the same blood. He is the only one capable of understanding them, that is, if he wants to. He has been the cause of the messy situation from the beginning and it is his responsibility to clear the air-not the responsibility of a friend. No matter what people say, a friend should be spared certain personal family secrets at times. This he learned from Grandma.

After deep concentration, Michael jumps up as if snapping out of a nightmare. "The Letter, where's the Letter?" He blurts out, nervously searching his pockets and removing everything around him.

"It's in my bag. Have you forgotten you gave it to me already?" asks Sheck, a little confused.

Michael snaps and starts to mumble, "No, you're lying. I want to see it." His fingers were now going through Sheck's bag.

"Give that to me." Sheck snatches the bag from Michael, becoming irritated, reaches deep inside, takes the letter, and waves it in Michael's face. "Here it is. Are you happy now?"

"Okay! Okay! But I beg of you, please, be careful with it. Don't lose it. You're the only person in our community whom I can trust. You know our people when they come abroad… Some are just too unreliable. All they're good at is gossiping, time and time again. I owe you one, Sheck….I owe you."

"You can count on me."

"Wait, I want to see it again, one last time."

Sheck doesn't argue. Again, he pulls the letter out of his bag and waves it under Michael's nose. Happy, Michael gets up, shakes his friend's hand, and hugs him while wishing him a safe and wonderful journey, over and over again.

Rambling, Michael makes his way to the door, stumbles on his helmet, then stands up immediately before quickly disappearing out the door. Sheck follows him to the bottom of the stairs and watches puzzled, as Michael retreats behind the handlebars of his bicycle. Sheck's head spins, difficult to understand that behind this apparently jovial guy, hides an enormous bag full of unsorted feelings. Back in his apartment, Sheck takes the letter out of the bag, handles it for awhile, thinking about whether or not to open it, changes his mind, and puts it back.

Michael peddles his way home, delighted to have delivered his precious package on time. It is past rush hour. The street is cleared. He pedals more slowly. Now, he can breathe, convinced that his painful past will be buried and forgotten, at last. He feels neither hatred, nor anger towards his parents, strangely. All he really wants is an explanation. He wants to know everything to give him peace of mind. He wants to know things about his past, his birth, his childhood, himself…Without them, he wouldn't be in this world as he is here now.

He feels that in his mother is the one to whom all the credit is due. A small change of heart on her part and Michael would not have been born. But she had made a promise to go on with the pregnancy against all odds. Was her part, thus, not yet done? Was he now being ungrateful for wanting to clarify the dark times of his past? He doesn't have the answer and shrugs.

The ball is in their court and up to them to play it now, his father, particularly. Michael is ready to get everything off his chest, a one-on-one talk with his father, from beginning to end, maybe some of the details would be omitted, but the essential would remain intact. He'd make sure of that. He would make sure they go back to the very beginning, where it all had begun...that summer in Belfast years ago.

The Encounter

North Belfast, April 1961. The weather was nice, neither cold nor hot much as those typical moments that also characterized the Irish Autumns, when trees started to wear their reddish outfits. Leaves slowly dropped. Various activities spread around the courtyard of the University of North Belfast.

It was almost six o'clock in the evening. The day had ended as usual with a briefing by the Dean of the Medical Department. The students remained seated to digest the final instructions before leaving. Anam, a young African student, was the last one to get up. He looked around to make sure he hadn't forgotten anything. As he was leaving, his professor called him over, "Mr. Anam! Would you be available to do your internship a little sooner than the others?" Anam looks perplexed. The dean, a bald middle-aged man with a strange accent characteristic of career long medical personnel, continues: "Tonight, for example, we have a tropical case at my private clinic. It's a common disease in the sub-Saharan countries. It would be a good opportunity for you to return to your roots -- what do you say?"

Before Anam had a chance to answer, the professor pretty much answered for him. "Anyway, you don't have much choice. When one chooses this profession, one does not have a choice too often; you can take my word for it."

Anam flashed a smile before asking his mentor, "What time is the operation scheduled for?"

His professor glanced at his watch. "You could come at ten o'clock. You need to get some rest. You'll need it, I'm sure."

After giving Anam a few more details, they parted company.

"You see, I always tell you, you'd make a good fortuneteller… you're so good at guessing. But this time you are wrong. The professor was telling me that you have to dissect a corpse tomorrow… and it's a guard from the throne of England, no less. What can be more exciting than this for an IRA man like you?"

"Ya bastard! Always have the last word." Mereck wanted to give his friend a pat on the back when his knapsack fell to the ground, scattering all of its contents about. Laughing uncontrollably, Anam let out one last sentence before leaving. "Chicken! He already shakes at the idea of dissecting a dead British soldier. What a shame!"

Mereck was looking for something to yell back but Anam was already on his moped. Like a bat out of hell, he barreled down the winding hill that leads to the campus. Mereck stared at Anam as he disappeared behind the building.

Since Anam's arrival in the country, two years ago, Mereck had been his only true friend. There were no boundaries to their friendship. They were like two brothers. One might say they even were a little too crude in their language with one another, but it was their way of doing things. Their wordplay sometimes became a little too daring.

Anam had been home fifteen minutes when Mereck finally arrived. He was out of breath and appeared to be a little on the defensive. Anam was busy cooking. Mereck went to his room without saying a word. They remained silent for quite a while. Once he was done in the kitchen, Anam hollered in the direction of Mereck's open door. "Come and eat, you shyster. I made your favorite meal."

Mereck jumped out of bed, screaming as loud as he could. "Wow! Groundnut stew again? I adore this dish."

"Lousy cooks adore all dishes, as far as I know."

Mereck didn't comment. He was already devouring his food.

A few minutes went by and then Anam suddenly got up and blurted out, "The last one washes the dishes!"

Mereck started to get up but changed his mind immediately. He knew it was too late. Anam was too quick for him. Mereck sat back to finish his meal while Anam was getting ready for his night shift schedule.

It was 9:45 p.m., when Anam arrived at the clinic. He made his way passed the long line up to the receptionist's desk. His elbows on the table, he gently asked for directions. Betty, the young brunette in her early-twenties, curly hair, beautiful face, snapped at him in a harsh and impatient voice, "I'm sorry, sir, but there are other patients ahead of you. If you could stand in line like everyone else I'll be delighted to help you when it is your turn."

A cynical smile on his face, Anam added, "I'm afraid I can't wait. I have an appointment with the Dean and I'm already late, madam."

"Don't call me "madam," sir." She composed herself and sharply said, "This is a hospital and everybody waits to see the doctor, whomever he is. Do you understand?" Anam takes a badge from his bag, hands it to Betty. "I'm Anam. I'm here to assist the Dean tonight…"

Before he could even finish his sentence, she was apologizing profusely. "Oh! I'm sorry, doctor. Why didn't you tell me earlier? The Dean's been expecting you," she said, pointing to the door across from her desk.

The other people waiting exchanged surprised looks. Before going into the office, Anam glanced again towards the secretary as she waves discreetly at him. And so began the connection: mind, body and soul between the young African medical student and the young medical secretary.

The following morning, Anam was jolted from his sleep by the telephone ringing. Half asleep, he groped around his bed for the receiver.

"Hello! Could I speak to Doctor Anam?"

"This is he, and who am I speaking to?"

"Doctor, it's me, Betty, the secretary at the clinic. Do you remember me? I was a little rude to you last night. I wanted to apologize for my behavior. It's really not what you think."

"Well, good morning, Betty. Don't worry about that, it happens to me all the time. I'm used to it now. And please call me Anam. I don't like the doctor title that much, only when I'm at the hospital."

Betty didn't say anything, and neither did he. An eternity seemed to pass before Anam broke the uncomfortable silence. "So, how are you doing, Betty?"

"Very well, and you?"

"Fine, thank you."

"I assure you Doctor… I mean, Anam -- I'm already forgetting that you don't want me to call you doctor. I assure you, it won't happen again -- Ah, when will you be assisting at our clinic again?"

"I'm afraid you'll be seeing me over there, every Thursday. I hope it doesn't bother you?"

"Not at all. And it'll let me make up for the way I treated you yesterday. I wouldn't want you to have a bad impression of Irish women."

"Please, don't change on my account. It's more interesting like this."

She laughed for a moment. "You're interesting, Doctor-I mean Anam. I look forward to seeing you again. I have a few patients waiting, I must say goodbye for now."

"Thank you for the call and have a good day!"

"Good day, Doctor… ah, have a good day, Anam."

As soon as he hung up, Anam runs into Mereck's room, excited, "You won't believe this... the secretary at the clinic... She just called me. I think I'm in love."

"My dear 'Valentino,' come back to earth, mate. This is not love. Every medical secretary dreams of going to bed with a doctor, sooner or later. And a black doctor...must be terribly exciting, don't ya think?" Mereck said, bursting into laughter.

"I'm serious. You know her....Tell me what she's like. No, don't," he took it back, quickly changing his mind. "It's not necessary. I know she is great. You can keep your opinion to yourself."

"Ya hardly know her and already you're crazy about her? Be careful, then. Secretaries like her... you'll meet a lot of them in your career."

"I don't need to know her. Back home, we don't fool around with marriage. You are given a woman to marry by your parents and you do it. And it always works."

"Good luck, if it's a question of culture. But promise me that no matter what, I'll always get my ground-nut stew with rice whenever I come to visit ya."

"That, you'll have to negotiate with her."

"I'll have warned ya." Anam rips the covers off Mereck, then runs into his own room before Mereck can catch him.

Days went by and the phone calls continued. Anam asked her on their first date the second time they saw each other at the clinic. She accepted, and their first date took place at Anam's apartment on an evening that Mereck had planned to spend the night out.

All the necessary arrangements had been made to ensure that the date would be memorable. A red candle was placed on the table. The lights were dim and dinner was spent in a warm ambiance.

Afterwards, Anam took Betty's hand. She didn't withdraw. She tightened her lips as he started to gently stroke the top of her hand back and forth. Her beautiful eyes, partially closed, sparkled. They breathed harder and harder, as if they had just walked up the stairs. Anam moved naturally closer and stood behind her. His hands caressed her shoulders and neck. She smiled, slowly tilting her head to the left and to the right, but with slight reservation. He invited her for a dance. The steps and the style in which they executed their dance were just for such a particular circumstance. When the music died, he invited her to his room. With a little hesitation, she followed him. He opened the door, gestured to let her in first, motioned closer from behind, closed the door, and hold her by the hips as they choreograph their steps towards the bed. Right by the bedside, he pulled her tightly towards him, dropped a gentle kiss on her neck. She slightly leaned over to give him more space around her ears. Gently, he started to rub her earlobe with his lips while his hands travel hesitantly, but slowly from under her skirt between her legs. She slowly squeezed them together at first, to stop his entry, and then released them to let his hands in as they moved into no man's land. Suddenly, their breath became one as their chests pound heavier and heavier. One after another, the soft fabrics started to hit the floor as they returned to the days of Adam and Eve. Behind the closed door, the pact was sealed on a new foundation for everlasting promise only new lovers know how to make.

  The following days were glorious. Not a day would go by where they wouldn't see or, at least, speak to each other. Every day he, after his classes, will jump on the phone to enquire about news from her and she, during working hours and after work, will highjack the phone for eternity. It was life at its best for the young African medical student. Love was at the rendezvous.

Walking alone, Anam smiled peacefully, glorifying the sky and the earth. He was happy. Things were going very well for him…and for them. The only barrier in their relationship was their color difference, but the only thing that mattered to Anam was their love -- not the color of their skin. And he surely wasn't going to let that get in the way.

Anam excelled at everything: Music, sports, academics, and now love -- his fields of undiminished excellence. His exploits were without boundaries. No one could measure up to him at the university shot-put competitions. Fame and glory were a part of him in everything he did. At school, he was at the top of his class. As a guitar player, he was selling out at the Afro-Cuban club where he performed with his band, 'Los Latitos.' Every weekend, Betty sat at the front table near the stage and get up and dance to every single number they played. She always made sure her darling Anam only had eyes for her. Love was in the air and the race towards total happiness, long aspire by new relations had just begun, and the participants were up to the challenge.

In the small clinic, the relationship between the African intern and the Irish medical secretary kept the rumor mill busy.

Three months went by.

April 1962 was the time Anam had chosen for the big jump. It was two o'clock p.m. and he was going door to door, shop to shop, on a famous street known for its high taste in wedding exhibitions. After looking for hours, he entered a special jewelry shop. Diamond rings were displayed everywhere. Anam looked around, smiling. He stood in the middle waiting for a salesman to help him. But no one did. He waited a few more minutes and then decided to leave. It was only when he was just about out the door when an Indian salesman approached him. "Sir! How can I help you?"

Anam hesitated and stopped. Walking away was not an option. He saw one in particular and who knows if he could find it elsewhere. "I want one of those rings, there."

"Ah, you are taking the big jump," the man said, teasingly.

Anam nodded and smiled ear to ear. The man walked behind the display and returned with the diamond ring in a gift box. Anam took it, pulled a different ring from his pocket and compared the two. He put the diamond on his pinky finger."

"We have other ones, ones without real diamonds and much less expensive," the salesman said as Anam continued to study the ring.

Anam looked up with a smile on his face. "No, I want this one."

The man's eyes were wide open. "The price… It's almost $800, sir!"

"I don't care about the price… you know what?"

"No," the vendor replied.

"When you love, things have no price."

"Words to live by." The vendor put the ring in the box in a hurry. Anam paid, shook hands with the man and with all the other employees and customers watching, he strolled across the shop and out the door.

A little while later Anam reached the clinic. The employees seemed to be looking at him in a peculiar way, as if they could feel the overwhelming energy in him. He rushed over to Betty's desk. She was not there. He calmly paced around as he normally did, waiting for her to return from the ladies' room.

Five and then ten minutes went by, but still no sight of her. He approached the girl who was sitting in her place. "Pardon me, Miss. Do you know if Betty is working today?"

The girl quickly answered, "Are you Doctor Anam?"

"Yes."

"Betty left this letter for you."

Anam took the envelope. Under the watchful eyes of some of the people around him, he went into his office and tore it open. The words were clear and concise:

My love!
I am sorry for not saying goodbye but I hope someday, you will understand. In the name of a love that united us and will continue to live in us until the end of time. Please, do not judge me. We so often say that the heart has its reasons, which reason itself ignores. My decision was based on very personal reasons. My leaving is the only alternative. Please don't try to go against destiny. It would be to no avail. Unfortunately, there are things in life we cannot change; we can only take them as is, with regret. I will be in touch with you again, at an appropriate time. Please don't resent me. One thing is sure; I will keep forever in my heart these past months together.
Take good care of yourself.
With love,
Your Betty.

Anam slumped into his chair. He took a few deep breaths. Quietly, he put the letter down on the table. "Not to resent you," he muttered.

Anam didn't know which saint to profess or even call upon. The blood in his veins was rushing. Suddenly, he felt an enormous feeling of shame. His eyes wandered in the direction of the partially opened office window. He wanted to see if anyone was spying on him. He was convinced those friends of hers had to know something about Betty's scheme. The feelings inside of him were clashing. Hatred or sadness, he could not define them. He asked himself all sorts of questions, going back in time, searching for a reason that would explain what happened, but he could not find anything. Everything was a blur. Powerless, he could only feel in his heart the big foundation on which he had been carefully laying brick after brick, collapse. He thought about the dynamic bond between atoms that maintain a body's balance. In all certainty, when this bond doesn't hold anymore, there is nothing we can do. The body, not unlike the soul, is destined to an ultimate end. The hand had been dealt, played, and he had to accept the outcome.

After what seemed to be an eternity of silence, Anam got up from his chair and paced the floor back and forth. For a very brief moment, he looked at Betty's picture that he always kept in his wallet. He was just about to sit down and start to work when there was a knock at the door. He jumped, the kind of jump that jolts you out of a nightmare; but he regained control of himself immediately. "Come in, it's open."

"Doctor, everything is ready for the operation," said a young nurse with a wide smile.

Anam smiled back with all the enthusiasm he could muster under the circumstances.

"Very well. I'll be with you in a minute."

Before he even finished his sentence, Anam had found his notebook and disappeared behind the doors of the operating room, almost at the same time as the nurse. The prescription was already set in his mind: not to show his personal problems, not displaying even the smallest inkling of emotion. This was imperative -- a question of custom! What a dishonor it would be to let people know that the woman you loved had abandoned you. The sentimental defections are a feature of our human nature….The wheel must continue to turn. Yes, a number of sick people can be saved, but some will also die right before his eyes and he will continue to practice his profession. Love will survive. Children will be born; some will die at birth, some will survive and so life goes on. These are the ingredients that make life so amazing. And not to accept what comes our way would be just wrong. Right?

"No! No!" Anam kept saying to himself on his way to the operation room. Succeed in this operation now and many more to come in the future; succeeding in what his country sent him for should be his first priority. At the same time, he was not ready to throw to the windows the opportunities life brought his way. He turned to the nurse once more to acknowledge her presence. She passed a gentle finger in her hair to expose her face. Anam smiled at the gesture. She smiled back as they entered the operating room almost at the same time.

Elsewhere, life continued its unyielding routine.

The Birth

It was two o'clock in the afternoon on an early fall day in 1962. The last rays of sunshine were as mercurial as in the summer. The hot winds from the sea filtered into the cabin through the half-closed windows. Betty woke up, shaken as if out of a nightmare. Again and again, she wondered if the last minute decision she made to immigrate to Canada was the right one.

The first week into the trip, she hadn't stopped vomiting. Even though the doctor had assured her it would go away, she couldn't see any improvement. In the second week, a more serious look by the doctor at her situation revealed the unthinkable: Betty was pregnant.

She rushed out of the office, ran to her cabin, and locked herself up for the rest of the day. What a load on her shoulders when she realized that a child was in the picture! As daunting as it was, her decision was simple. With or without any help, she would do everything in her power to keep the child. It was a personal commitment, one she made in the name of love. A few years ago, she dreamed of leaving in search of adventure. Now the dream was materializing. She didn't have the choice. To let the opportunity of the Canadian dream slip away one more time would have been a death sentence with her father. At this, she thought of Anam, and hoped that one day he would understand and forgive her for what she did. The memory was strong enough to drag her back on the boat deck. Slowly but surely, she walks towards the cold structure of steel, staring into the horizon.

Betty closed her eyes, took a deep breath, reached into herself, and drifted back to that time in her life, and soon she started to cry. A gentle old lady to whom she had told the entire story, approached to comfort her. To appear somewhat composed, she crossed her arms and started to walk up the deck. Holding back the tears, Betty looked above at the sky, contemplating the stars as if they carried a message she needed to interpret at that particular moment. Beneath, happy passengers, held to the safety rails with iron grips, and studied the vast body of salt water as the monster structure of metal cut through with ease. Betty broke into tears.

    Once again, she regained control of herself very quickly. With the back of her hand, she wiped her eyes. She reflected on the time when she was seventeen years old. Her first pregnancy was nearly to term and she had just completed high school. She still didn't understand how this horrible thing could have happened to her. She kept searching and to this day, she still didn't understand how and when this pregnancy originated with all the precautions she had taken. Yes! Why is it always so easy for her to get pregnant while other women would die for it in vain?

    Her father, a staunch Baptist, swore under all the heavens that any newborn child must have a mother and father who are together in matrimony. She searched, deeply, but could not find out, even now, who could have been the father of her first child. She only knew that she was his mother. Hard in such circumstances to broadcast that you want the best for your child, even harder, if you're of the Baptist faith and Irish. Unable to accept her situation, her father kicked her out of the house in a violent rage. A family friend welcomed Betty.

    Months later, the child was born. The baby's grandmother braved her husband's bitterness and took back Betty and her new born into their home. She thus adopted her grandchild and liberated Betty from all her responsibilities. Free, Betty enrolled in a medical secretary program and obtained her diploma a year later. A few weeks went by before luck again came knocking on Betty's door offering her a secure position in one of the most affluent clinics of North Belfast.

Attracted by the fashion of the moment and looking for adventure, Betty swore she would leave like everybody else. At first, her plans for immigration were a bit of a joke. She didn't really believe she would go through with it, but when she saw that the entire city was leaving, she seriously committed to leaving as well and for good. At any cost, she promised herself.

Then came along Anam and she fell in love again. Another trap she had vowed to never fall into. What else could she have done when she received the immigration document? She opted to keep it secret. It was essential that she didn't let herself be charmed by the notion of love again. The situation became even more complicated, when their relationship deepened day after day. She was already aware of the consequences and she didn't want to play that game another time. Besides, she didn't want to ever regret not having grabbed a chance and blame someone for having been the reason. More importantly, counting on her mother again was out of the equation. She made it through passing for a sister with her own son under the same roof all those years, but not twice around. Her mother had done enough for her. Too much, maybe. The time had come for her to take responsibility for her own actions. Of course, circumstances like this create so many doubts in one's mind. But at this particular time, she felt headstrong and ready to face the hard reality of life: she was an immigrant discovering her land of asylum. And she was with child.

The days went by, painful and melancholic. Two weeks at sea had seemed like an eternity. On the fifteenth day, at precisely midnight, the ship entered the harbor. Her feet numb, Betty drug one after the other up to the custom's desk and then over to the immigration desk. Tired, she collapsed into an armchair in the middle of the waiting room. Her two suitcases and handbag lay there next to her. She searched in the outside pocket of one of the suitcases and took out a wrinkled piece of paper. The address for the women's shelter that a friend had given her was hardly legible. Straining her eyes, she deciphered the address one letter at a time. She jumped, when the immigration official called her name on the loudspeaker. Once the formalities with the immigration agent were over, she exited the harbor and called for a taxicab.

"223 Church Street," she threw at the driver. The driver placed the suitcases into the trunk, and then quickly put the car in motion. It was nearly two o'clock in the morning, but the main street leading from the harbor to downtown was packed with cars.

It is mid-April 1962, and Betty was getting in touch with her new home, Toronto, Canada. She had so many questions about this city, praised by so many people back in Belfast. The atmosphere, the air, the wind, everything she saw and felt about Toronto excited her curiosity more than anything else at that moment. Really, deep inside, it was not so much the fear of the unknown that frightened her, but rather the sensation that was growing in her stomach and traveling to her hips and all along her spinal column. This constant reminder was forcing her to pay the strictest of attention to every small detail parading before her.

About ten minutes into her journey, her mouth started to water and she started to feel nauseous. She asked the driver to stop. She opened the car door and threw up profusely. Then, the driver took off again, disgusted. A funny kind of smile distorted the face of the driver. "Is this your first time in Toronto?" he asked her.

"Yes." She answered without enthusiasm.

"Don't worry, you will adore this place. Church Street is very lively, especially at night."

"I don't doubt it. It's past midnight and you would think it's mid-day by the number of people that are out on the street."

"You know, young lady, life is always different from one place to another. I have been in all the big cities in this country and I can tell you that life here is good, except there's too much dishonesty. People have no heart here," said the driver, busting out into laughter.

"It's like that in all big cities," Betty said.

This opened up the opportunity for the driver to tell Betty the story of his life, from his clandestine passage at the Romanian border, through Belgium, Australia, Mexico, United States and finally into Canada. She tried to listen, but her mind was elsewhere. She thought instead of the things she had left behind in Ireland.

Betty was searching within herself, looking for the answer as to whether or not she had made the right choice, but it was too late, anyway. She had to accept her new life, and was trying to find a word, a phrase, a small comforting excuse to give herself, when the driver announced the end of the journey.

"Here is 223 Church. That will be twenty dollars please," he said, turning off the meter.

"Twenty?" Betty questioned.

"Okay. Give me ten. I'll take it because of you," he said, laughing. The car had stopped before a decrepit building. He attempted to comfort her, "You still have your whole life ahead of you. A little courage and everything will turn out for the best. That's what the adventure is all about." Betty wasn't listening anymore. All she wanted was to settle her fare and leave.

She grabbed her two suitcases and wobbled towards the reception area. The nightshift security guard, a young male from Haiti, welcomed her from his desk. She showed him her identification and he proceeded to leaf through a registry.

"Oh, you're the lady from Belfast," he said. "We were expecting you. You have room number 339." The security guard followed with a string of questions that always seemed to be asked of people just arriving in their new country. When he was finished, he added, "The stairs, over this way." He pointed his finger in her direction. "My name is Fritz. If you need anything at all, don't hesitate to ask me."

"The suitcases, could you give me a hand?" asked Betty.

Fritz escorted her to the door. From then on, she would be known as "the lady in room 339." For whatever service, her room number was the only reference needed. That rule was clear.

Betty was happy to have a roof over her head, but deep inside she would've preferred a flat like the one she had just left behind. She swore she would find a job as quickly as possible and leave this place, even if she didn't have a clue about what life had in store for her. Time… she needed plenty of time to heal all the wounds and recreate herself all over again. But right now, a good night's sleep was what she felt she truly needed.

Two weeks later, Betty found work in a small clinic on the outskirts of town. The commuting distance was considerable and the salary rather small, but she couldn't wait to be independent. A month later, she moved out of the shelter.

Winter had kept its appointment. Now, a car was what Betty needed. Standing at the bus stop in the cold weather was difficult, especially with the extra weight of the coat resting on her spine, her swollen feet, and all the discomforts of the pregnancy. She eventually found a car and bought it. It didn't have a functioning heater, but it was all her budget would allow.

The big adventure had begun. Winter had arrived with its full audacity. Betty sought the comfort of blankets both in her bed and in her car. She didn't have a choice; otherwise, she'd freeze her toes and fingers. As for her stomach, it was forever growing. She sometimes wondered if twins might even be nesting in there. No sooner had the thought entered her head, when she chased it away. It was entirely out of the equation to even have such a negative thought. Yes, she wanted this child, but certainly not twins.

Her life would be completely ruined, and just the thought of it made her sick. She only wanted to live and enjoy her new life.

One evening as Betty was returning home from work, her car broke down. Jeremiah, a bald bank teller in his late thirties, with good manners, stopped to offer his help. He couldn't believe it when he found out that her car didn't have a heater. Betty told him it had only stopped working that morning. He insisted she not drive the car again, until she got it fixed.

Betty was not comfortable with the idea of going with a stranger, but had no other choice. Two tow trucks showed up and the drivers got into an argument as to which one of them was going to take the car. Jeremiah gave the address of a garage to the winning tow truck driver and paid the bill, while Betty waited in his car. When he returned, she insisted that she didn't want to be indebted to anyone, but her words were the farthest things from the man's ears. Calmly, he waited for the end of her speech and asked if he could take her home, which he did. Before leaving, he made sure she was all right and promised to drive her every day for as long as she didn't have her car. Since then, Jeremiah became the man for all circumstances, and he easily conquered her heart. A unique friendship developed between the two of them. His generosity left her feeling slightly embarrassed, but the relationship made her happy. He looked after her needs, helping whenever possible and always making sure mother and child were growing healthy together.

On February 24, 1962, a child was born. They named him Michael Deh Anam. When Betty came out of the hospital, a generous surprise awaited. A new apartment to go with the new baby. The place was filled with flowers and balloons floated everywhere. Jeremiah was nervous, but worked up enough courage to ask, "Betty, do you want to be my wife?"

"Yes," she answered as tears of joy flowed.

But only God knows what lies beneath.

Days went by. The emotions eased with the time. Then, came the moment of truth: To find a solution for the unwanted baby. The happiness that comes with love had won over the joy of childbirth. The second has lasted for only a brief moment. It was time to find a place for Michael, if love was to survive. He polluted the atmosphere and prevented life from following its regular, true course- from Jeremiah's point of view.

Ten months had gone by and it was a too much for Betty's lover. A solution had to be found and quickly. There were two alternatives: give up Michael for adoption or send him to his father, but what could a foreign student do, alone with a newborn in his care? Adoption was the best recourse, Betty decided, so she wrote a short letter to the father to explain the situation. It was clear and concise, with every word carefully chosen:

Dear Anam,

I am informing you that you are the father of a handsome little boy. His name is Michael Deh. See? I even put your last name on his certificate. He is ten months old. He is beautiful and dear but I want you to help me find a solution for him. Do you remember the conversation we had one day about adoption? You told me you were in favor of the idea. I believe that the moment has come for us to choose this alternative. Michael will have a better life with adoptive parents. I am at a turning point in my life and this decision is forcing itself upon me. I need you to understand. I'll wait for your reply.

Farewell!
Betty M.

The Diplomatic Package

It was eight o'clock. Anam had just returned home from the clinic when he found the mail. That handwriting, he could recognize it among any others. The postmark indicated that the letter had been mailed from Canada seven days ago. Without any doubt, he knew whom the letter was from, so he promptly tore open the envelope, eager to find out what was inside. The information was both marvelous and disheartening.

"No! No! And, no!" he swore.

The request contained in the letter was not one he would ever consider. He was a charitable man and had given generously to many, for God's sake, but never, never would he be able to give up his child for adoption. He sighed. Circumstances had split him and Betty up but he was still in love with her and was ready to forgive her. So why not marry her and have a family life together?

Anam recognized an opportunity to put order back into this situation of chaos. He picked up the telephone and quickly dialed the phone numbers in the letter. The male voice at the other end took him by surprise, but he did not allow himself to be jealous over it. In his deep African voice, he said, "May I speak to Betty, please?"

"One moment please," answered the voice.

Jeremiah covered the mouthpiece of the telephone before calling Betty, "Honey! It's for you... I think its Michael's father." She motioned for him to go into the other room. Jeremiah obliged. After a few seconds, Betty put the receiver to her ear.

"Hello," she said in a cold voice. This was an awkward moment.

"How are you… and the baby?" quickly asked the father.
"He is doing very well. Did you receive my letter?"
"As you can see, I did."
"I beg of you, please don't be angry with me. I cannot keep him with me. Please understand."
"I understand, Betty. Betty, please come back. We can start over again. We will get married and raise this child and others together. We will be a family."
"Please don't complicate the situation. You know, that's impossible. I just need your help to finalize the adoption papers, okay?"
"Adoption is out of the question. I would rather take him to my mother. That is what my people do. Give me some time to contact her and I'll get back to you within the next few days."
"The sooner the better it will be for everyone involved."
"Betty, I said I understand and I'll get back to you shortly, I will."
Anam stayed silent at his end. Betty waited a few seconds, and then hung up.

Three days later, he called back. The decision was to bring Michael to his grandmother and special arrangements were made with the embassy of Ghana, his father's birthplace. Consent had been given by the high commission to send the baby under diplomatic escort but in a special way: 'Diplomatic Package' was the ideal label found for Michael. So original! A special itinerary was chosen so the father would be able to see his son between two flights: Ottawa to London then Accra.

The day had arrived for Michael. His mother had decided to travel without Jeremiah to the embassy. She was discovering for the first time, and with her son, Ottawa, the capital of her haven country.

The air seemed a little cooler during this, the beginning of fall. Betty pulled the stroller. Her mind was elsewhere. Where? It was difficult to tell. As innocent as he was, Michael kept smiling and moving in his cradle, unaware of the plot against him and his destiny. He had finished taking his milk, and as always, he was smiling and making faces.

It was 4 o'clock when mother and son arrived at the embassy. The employees were all around Michael, admiring him. The social worker, a chubby man in his late forties, arrived a few minutes later. Betty had only ten minutes left to spend with Michael. The time had come to ship the "Diplomatic Package." He had to be taken to the airport as quickly as possible for the final formalities. This was the crucial moment for sharing the last feelings between mother and son. There was nothing more noble or intense than this. After all, this was the person which she had given life to. Betty was trying hard to remain dignified but the emotions were too strong, and the young women who worked at the embassy couldn't contain their tears. Betty was shivering from head to toe. Betty hadn't thought this whole thing would be so complicated. Michael was rather amused by all of the goings-on around him. He had been smiling since their arrival at the embassy. Happily, he reacted to everything with laughter. Betty tried not to show too much emotion. She forced a smile back to Michael, but the situation was too much, and her eyes quickly filled with overflowing tears.

It was 4:30 p.m. Time to say goodbye. The youngest passenger on flight 677 seemed to be taking everything quite well. He was smiling ear to ear when the flight attendant took him out of his cradle. Unable to contain her emotions, Betty turned her head to avoid meeting those eyes, seeing that look of innocence. Michael let out small sounds, trying to get her attention, trying to call her through the doorway.

As soon as Michael disappeared behind the doors with the flight attendant and the assigned escort, Betty burst into tears. She then composed herself and with assured and confident steps, walked towards the nearest telephone and dialed. At the first ring, a voice at the other end answered. Betty cried out, "Honey, I shipped the baby!" Everyone stopped to look at her. Embarrassed, she slammed down the receiver and fled the embassy as fast as she could.

Flight 677 departed for London at 6 o'clock. A few minutes later, Michael was asleep. He woke up two hours later and disrupted the calmness of this transatlantic flight. Did he realize what was happening to him? He cried incessantly and no consoling hand could calm him down. The passengers began asking questions and soon became aware of the circumstances surrounding him. Their emotions were divided: Some were repulsed. Others were compassionate. For the tender hearts, each one of his screams was like a sword piercing their soul. Many volunteered to help the flight attendants trying comfort the child. One by one, they all failed. Finally, an old Asian woman in her late sixties approached. No one understood the words that she mumbled, except for Michael. To him, they must have seemed perfectly clear. He started to smile. The woman picked him up from his cradle and everyone applauded. The compassionate hand had finally been found. They could now continue their flight in peace, at least, for a little while.

The day before, Michael's father had traveled from Belfast to London to see his son between Michael's two connecting flights. Anam didn't want to miss the only one opportunity by arriving late, so he left early. For two hours, Michael's father waited at the airport. He didn't want to miss this unique opportunity to be with his first child. He would not have another one until after his graduation. Maybe never.

After the eight-hour flight, father and son were together at last. but Anam's happiness wasn't shared. Michael was resisting, bracing his little body. He would have preferred being in the arms of the person of his choice. Amused, the Asian lady offered her hand. But the father was frustrated, and insisted on holding the baby. Michael started to protest with more wailing that soon translated into distress. Unable to control the situation, his father handed him back to the stranger. At the same moment, the officials announced the meeting had come to an end. The time had come for Michael to continue on his journey.

The Pancake Boy

It was 2'o clock p.m., when the plane landed. Michael had arrived on African soil. The hot tropical wind, mixed with the uproar of the airport, had unleashed a new crisis. This time it was difficult to give baby Michael all the attention he needed. First, the State had to transfer all the responsibilities to his new family. When all was in order, Michael was handed over to his new guardian and her accomplices. They came in a large number to welcome the one that comes from the far end of the world.

The welcoming was triumphant. The entire African family was present: grandmother, uncles, aunts, cousins, nephews and nieces, and everyone else with whatever title that might fit for the occasion. But Michael was not ready to stop crying, and he didn't seem to care about anybody. Every time he changed hands, he would scream louder. They were passing him around, looking for the one who could comfort him best. It was total panic. Suddenly, all calm returned, when grandmother took him in her arms. The entire gathering sighed a loud sigh of joyful relief. Michael's eyes went from one face to another, wondering probably about the new coloring around him. Ah, a baby's mind!

What a relief! What a dilemma! Michael was more than confused, but content or maybe too tired to cry. The difference in time and space was as clear as the sound and the ambiance at the airport. It was like he knew he couldn't win the psychological warfare. It was time to cooperate. And he did. With Michael on the same page with his new family, the journey resumed. The feelings that accompany the new procession along the main street that leads from the airport to the town center of the capital Accra was very mixed.

Ghana was less than a decade old as a country. A new chapter had just begun after the independence was given to its people by the British in 1957. Life had a whole meaning contrary to where Michael was from. Here, only a few streets were paved. The main road connecting the airport to downtown was one of them. What a joy for the delegation that came from the far away countryside to welcome Michael! Impressive were the images parading through the opposite side of the charter bus, snaking through Accra towards Michael's final destination. The architecture here has nothing comparable to the high-rise buildings from where he was coming from. The differences between the North and the South were well encrypted in life itself. The houses are very small. One could have believed they had all been designed by the same builder. Most of them have no cement or aluminum roof.

Michael was very quiet and careless. His eyes rolled left and right as if all these images meant something to him. No one could tell exactly what goes on in his mind.

Since the independence, the rush from the villages to the capital in search of a better life had created a clash of classes in the capital. Once, survival instinct had defined where you would belong. Now, the fortunate and visionaries have managed to create businesses of their own. Along the main boulevard, merchants improvised stands showcasing their latest acquisitions, ready to be turned over for cash. Young girls and boys parade along, with trays of local drink and gourmets to offer passengers in cars and passers-by.

One hour later, when the car hit the rugged road just a few minutes away from Accra, Michael reasserted his presence, quickly Grandma Antima handed him a piece of her famous pancake. Michael started to bite at it, and quickly become quiet.

The mission was materializing: grandmother was becoming a mother again.

Antima was fifty-five years old and mother of five children, two girls and three boys. Yoba, the eldest son was a farmer. As a youngster, he had difficulty focusing on his schoolwork. As a result, he failed to receive his primary school certificate and his father, upset, sent him far away into the farming area to one of his uncles to work on the farm.

Anam, the second child, was given a golden opportunity by his mother's older sister. She took it upon herself to explain to the father the benefits of pursuing post-secondary studies. After one brilliant year of studies in medicine at the University of Accra, Anam received a scholarship to study sports medicine in Belfast.

Wafouê, the third child, the favorite son to some accounts, chose the priesthood. For many years, he enjoyed honor and respect in the community, but things deteriorated, when he abandoned his ecclesiastic status to live a secular life. No one really knew the reason for this change of heart. His mother was shocked but accepted his choice in the end. Wafouê quickly assumed a normal life again as a literature professor. His habits when it came to women, however, were less than desirable. Not a month would go by without Antima having to summon the help of her nephew, a judge, to stifle paternity suits against him. Twenty-two years old and Wafouê had known enough women to build a small harem! Some contributed his bad character to those years *lost* in the seminary.

Awa and Ana were the fourth and fifth to be born. Both of them became pregnant following the sixth grade and assumed the role of stay-at-home mothers, much to the family's chagrin. Nevertheless, they seemed to be happy with their lives, even with nothing, and that's what Michael was about to experience.

After a few hours of driving, Michael was home. Lafaye was a small village amid the dense forest region in the west of Ghana. Near the border region of their neighboring country Ivory Coast and ninety miles outside of Accra, it had a population of less than one thousand people. A small market place divides the village from North to South. There's no electricity, no running water, no indoor toilets, no hospital, or whatever luxuries of life Michael could have partaken in from his birthplace was certainly nowhere to be found here. In contrast, there was a school with six classrooms; one thing of which the country was very proud. People from Ghana used to brag that, while the French colonials were building hotels in their neighboring country Ivory Coast, their counterpart, the British were building schools in Ghana. Just yet another chapter in the African continent legacy. Michael was home definitively and there was no turning back, at least not for the moment. Now, a new chapter of his life, with Grandma by his side, had started.

  The life journey of Grandma Antima was one- of-a-kind, a woman of all trades. From soap making to clothing, the pancake business had thrived for the past two decades. She was burdening herself yet overcoming every obstacle. And there were many that destiny had in store for her. Her pancake business was the only lucrative activity that she had to help her raise her children. She had done it for years before and she would continue to do it as long as she had the strength for it, even with a child in the picture. As usual, she would arise early in the morning, only now to schedule her day around baby bottles, diapers, and all the necessary chores she had long forgotten about.

  "*Once a mother always a mother*," she whispered to herself. It's part of the culture for grandparents to care for their offspring's kids. For anything in the world, Grandma Antima was not ready to change her daily routine, except to count on Michael in the picture from now on.

Five o'clock in the morning. It was day one for Michael on African soil. He was enjoying a good early morning sleep after the torment of jet lag, when Grandma Antima pulled him from the bed they share with Grandpa Adina. As for grandpa, even though he was not at the airport to welcome Michael due to old age, he was as excited as everyone else to see Michael.

It was time for Grandma Antima to get ready for business. She bathed Michael, fed and dressed him against his will, then placed him in a sling on her back with all the necessary precautions. With her left hand, she juggled to balance a large pot of ground flour on her head that she will use to make pancakes later. Her right hand held a jug of water to which a small oil lamp was attached. As soon as she felt comfortable enough, she was on her way to the market place. She needed good business and so she hurried to make sure she would secure a prime spot in the marketplace.

Michael was struggling with all his might to get out of the backpack contraption, but each time he tried to shout he would choke. He was finding himself in this uncomfortable position for the first time and he didn't like it at all. He stretched, grabbed, and fought to get his arms and legs out. His grandmother had to periodically lean her body to the left or to the right just to keep him in position. Michael started to scream, but this wasn't a good time for grandmother to help him. She was too busy rushing herself to work. He would have to get used to this position until he could walk on his own. Until then, he would spend his time in the backpack, taking in the surroundings, the air, the wind, and everything else around that his child mind would learn to adapt to. How easy for the child's mind to adapt so easily to situations!

Four years went by and Michael and Antima had become perfect accomplices. Every morning they rose together, followed their morning routine, as they would walk to the marketplace. Michael would lead the way, holding the jug of water on his head with his left hand and carrying the oil lamp in his right hand. Michael was always present in Antima's daily activities. He quickly developed an interest in them.

From time to time, when he was left alone to sell the last pancakes, some village boys would come by and tease him. Then one day, one boy went too far and stole one of his grandma's pancakes. Furious, Michael lunged at him and kicked him repeatedly. Luckily, passersby intervened just in time to free the boy from Michael's rage. Since that day, no one dared to bother him anymore. And he would forever be known as the "Pancake Boy". But whoever dared to call Michael by this name had better be ready for the fight of his life.

The First Day of School

September 1968, Michael was 6 years old. The time had come for him to go to school. His excitement was at its best on this day, the first morning of school, and Michael was happier than ever anticipated. He was singing, as he got ready. He learned that it was because of school that his father was able to go abroad. What else did he need to know? School is what he needed and wanted.

He put on his brand new shoes purchased for school and only that. Michael wiggled his toes, and started to walk around the room to make sure they fit well. They have to. Antima watched nodding in amazement, from her special armchair in the corner as usual, as Michael put on a brand-new khaki suit. Happily, he smoothed down every part of his clothes to perfection.

Grandma got up, went in the room, returned with a bag still wrapped in a package. Oh! What a surprise when grandmother held up the backpack in front of Michael, stating, "This is from your father. He sent it to you from abroad." Michael smiles from ear to ear as always when his grandma mentioned his father abroad. He never asked questions about them. Nobody knew and nobody wondered to ask him, not before and not now. He was convinced his father and mother were somewhere over there thinking about him. He was overjoyed. His new bag on his back, he was ready to go. Soon, his cousin, Adjobi, joined him. He tried to hold Michael's hand, but Michael was too difficult to control with all the excitement consuming him.

The news spread very quickly. At school, all the children had gathered around him. Everyone wanted to touch his beautiful bag that had come from so far away. They had never seen one like it before. The curiosity and interest in this foreign item was enormous, and Michael was delighted in showing off his possession. Deep down in his heart, the one thing that gave him the most pleasure was not the thought of his parents and how wonderful they were to send him this gift that was attracting so much attention, but how he could follow his father's footsteps by doing well like him at school and go abroad one day.

  The bell rang at 8 o'clock, precisely. All the children were instructed by the headmaster to line up in an orderly manner, according to class level. Assisted by teachers and parents, the children quickly complied. Michael stood in front of the first grade class, just like his cousin had told him to. The teacher was already in position, and a few minutes later took the class list out of his pocket and began the roll call. The same scenario was repeated for each of the six classes. The teacher was a bald man, and Michael found him very intriguing. He looked around at the other children to see their expression, but they all seemed to be paying attention to everything else around them except for the teacher. The bell rang. The children waited for their names to be called out and one by one, they climbed the few steps leading up to their appointed classroom, eyes fixed onto the floor.

  Boys and girls took their respective spots. Michael was the tenth pupil to be called in. When he entered, a small girl in the first row moved over slightly and made room for him. Without hesitation, he jumped at the chance. Ten minutes later, everyone was seated and the classroom was completely full. As soon as the teacher came in, a dead silence reigned in the room. He walked between the rows of desks, laying down his hand on the heads of the children who had not combed their hair as he walked between the ranks.

Those lucky enough not to have received a hand stroke over the head were rather amused by the scene. Michael didn't seem intimidated at all. He patted down his hair, smiled to himself with confidence as he remembered his grandma's advice, "First impression is key."

A mixture of laughter and cries were the signs announcing the first day of school. When the teacher finally spoke, the students were remarkably attentive. Every word coming from his mouth was a melody to Michael's ears. Michael was more than attentive and had an enormous desire to go to school. The school that would one day enable him to take a plane and be together with his father and mother, like his grandma always sang to him. That first day of school was the shortest day Michael had ever known.

On the way home, Michael thought about something that he'd never had to think about before his skin color. He always thought he was like everybody else, but this was not an opinion shared by all. He was a different child and he had to admit it and learn to live with it. In addition, he was starting to feel stifled by the preferential treatment given to him by some teachers.

As time went by, Michael started to see clearly that he was a case apart. He was spared from receiving the strap, fetching water and wood at noon on the first Friday of every month, as was the general rule in the village school. Michael didn't complain at all. He loved it.

When his skin color became an issue, he was always ready to defend himself. Sometimes not a day would go by without a fight between Michael and some other students. Even with all this turmoil in his young life, Michael continued to progress from one class to the other under the approving eyes of his teachers, and most important of all, he didn't disappoint his grandmother who was always there, standing tall, in the first row, applauding his every graduation.

A little too tall for his age, he would make his way, with great pride and honor, up to the podium. Once, his grandma shouted his name so loudly that he stumbled, but that did not stop her. Michael finally got accustomed to her style, her special display of love. There was no way of stopping her.

The First Connection

The years were going by. Michael was 9 years old and in his fourth year of elementary school when his father had sent him a long letter, enclosed with a plane ticket. Antima was not happy at all to let her beloved grandson go, but she submitted herself to the will of her son. She announced the news to Michael, who was ecstatic at joining his parents abroad.

At school, everyone soon found out that Michael would not be one of them anymore following the January school break. His friend Éliane was sad. She is the very first one who made space for him his first day of school. Michael comforted her and promised he would ask his father to send for her too. Éliane smiled, her good humor returned and they resumed their fun.

A week later, Michael's plane landed at the Belfast International Airport on December 20, 1969. A flight attendant escorted him to the arrival lounge, where she said something into a loud speaker that Michael hardly understood except for the name Anam. He realized then she was speaking about him. What a strange accent to Michael. He shook his head and smiled.

A few minutes later, a couple approached him with two small girls. Michael noticed their complexion was the same as his. The gentleman looked like one of his uncles who lived in the village. The man, as a welcoming gesture, ruffled Michael's hair, patted his back and pulled him close to him. Anam's wife, Florence, a white woman, like his biological mother as he was told, was beautiful and charming at first sight as she moved closer to them. She stooped down to Michael's level and looked into his eyes. For a moment, Michael thought she was going to take him in her arms, but to his surprise, she shook his hand instead, repeating several times.

"Hello, Michael! How are you?"

Michael didn't have the time to answer as Michael's father introduced the two little girls as his sisters, Jennifer and Laura. They were six and four years old, respectively. They looked at each other with the inquisitive eyes of children seeing each other for the first time.

"Let's go home!" said Michael's father.

Michael started the walk, even though he did not know where he was going. By the time they had reached the parking structure, tears were coming down his cheeks. The coat they had just put on him weighed a ton on his shoulders, he was dragging his feet, and was having a difficult time tolerating the cold wind sweeping his face. Michael was craving the hot weather of the home he'd left behind. He really felt as if he was in another world, far away from his real home.

On the way home, Michael marveled at the tall glass houses and their windows reflecting the sun's shining rays. For a moment, he forgot about everything and admired all the happenings on the streets. He laughed when he saw Santa Claus parading near an intersection, and gestured to attract the attention of his two sisters saying, "Look! Look! Father Christmas! Father Christmas!" Michael was the only one yelling. Furious, Florence lashed out, "Be quiet, Michael! We are not in the bush here!"

Michael quickly retreated into himself. He felt strange and out of place, and he didn't say a word until they reached home. The car parked in front of a nice two-story house in an upper class neighborhood. Michael stood at the front door, wide-eyed in wonderment at how magnificent the house was. He had never seen anything like it in his little village, but he didn't dare express his feeling of amazement openly. From now on, every gesture he made would be calculated, mentally rehearsed and carefully examined, before delivering it to the world around him. He would discreetly check to see if anyone was looking before touching any object in the house. The Christmas decorations were particularly exciting to him. Michael walked around the tree, silently admiring everything.

His parents went upstairs. Laura took Michael's hand and showed him around the house. A short while later, she said to him, "My mom said that if I'm a good girl, Santa Claus will come into my room and put a big present next to my bed."

"Who is Santa Claus?" asked Michael.

His sentence hardly finished, Laura turned to her sister and asked, "Jennifer, who is Santa Claus?"

"How many times do I have to tell you that I don't know who Santa Claus is, but you keep asking me the same question?" Before Jennifer could finish her sentence, she walked into her room and slammed her door shut.

Undisturbed by her sister's outburst, Laura proceeded, "If you don't sleep, you'll get to see him. I'm not lucky… I always fall sleep before he gets here. Do you believe that this is the reason why Jenny doesn't like me? You know, she is very mean… If you don't sleep, you'll really see him."

Laura pulled Michael by the arm as she continued talking. He followed her asking no questions. They stopped at the door to her room. She opened it and ushered Michael in. He was so astonished that he unconsciously pulled his hand away from Laura's. He moved from one object to the next, examining each one with the utmost interest. Not one single item was overlooked. Michael was both surprised and puzzled to see the little girl's room. As far as he knew, children didn't have their own room, at least not where he came from. Her hands on her hips, Laura watched her brother. After a while, wanting to satisfy his curiosity, Michael walked towards Laura. "Is this your room?"

"Yes!"

"Wow! Aren't you afraid to sleep all alone in here?"

"I am not afraid. It's Jennifer who always wants to sleep in mom and dad's room. Do you want to see Jennifer's room? Come on," said Laura, pulling Michael by the arm to follow her.

He was a little hesitant, but he finally gave in. To their surprise, Jennifer's room was locked, and she refused to open the door.

Determined, Laura started to pound on the door as hard as she could. "Open the door, Jennifer....Open the door!" she kept shouting as she kicked and banged on her sister's door.

She started to cry after a few minutes. Her mother heard and hurried out of her room.

"What did you do to her?" she shouted at Michael, her eyes piercing him.

Michael's heart was pounding. He couldn't understand what he was being accused of. He had just arrived and already had been through two humiliating incidents. He didn't know what was going on. He felt a certain panic inside of him, starting in his belly. He answered, not really knowing what to say exactly.

"It wasn't me. I didn't do anything," he pleaded.

"Oh, it wasn't you? Go back to the living room before I get really angry," she shouted as loud as she could.

She ran back to the room where her husband was and slammed the door. "I told you I wouldn't be able to tolerate this situation. That child has hardly set foot in this house and he is going through everything, snooping around all the rooms. Honestly, he's getting on my nerves."

"Please, Florence. Are you telling me he's already getting into mischief? He just got here. Give him a chance."

"I haven't reprimanded him for anything yet, but you know how I feel. I don't want him to disturb my children."

"We had an agreement. He can't find out that you're not his mother. Please try to control yourself. He is still young and I don't want him to know that his biological mother sent him to his grandmother like some package. You are his mother. Is that clear?"

Her arms dropped, a sign of her discouragement, "I don't know. This is going to be much harder than I thought."

Anam didn't say another word. He stood up and walked over to his wife, took her into his arms and gave her a loving hug. They stayed like this for a long time. A bond was created, but how sincere was it?

Time passed and Michael was constantly berated for everything he did. As usual, he would hide in his little corner and blame himself. He just didn't know how to be good like his two sisters. He tried hard to copy them but he just couldn't get it. He is a village child and nothing would change that.

The happiness of their coming together was very brief. In Michael's mind, everything was vague and unclear. He continued to receive his daily share of reprimands and scolding. By some kind of curse, life made sure he would not live one single day without some stern punishment, either ordered by the wife or executed by the father or vice versa. The worse was always putting the blame on her husband. And every time it happened, there was no room for compromise between Michael and his father. The wall of ice that had started to grow between them has reached exponentially high levels beyond reason. It would break for a moment and then rise higher than none could have ever imagined. The griping would rise to a high pitch until the victim himself cracked. When he would start to cry, they would send him to his room -- the torture chamber -- for the rest of the day.

One evening, things between Michael and his mother were actually positive. She was asking him a lot of questions about his old school and about life with his grandmother. Michael was proud to tell her how he had become the star of his school because of his backpack, and recalled how he ran after the children who mocked him when he was selling pancakes with Antima. He told her about his soccer games. Unfortunately, the honeymoon was soon over, when, overwhelmed by the excitement, he accidentally knocked a glass onto the floor, smashing it into little pieces. First, he had to endure a torrent of insults, and then was sent to his room for the rest of the day. There, sitting on his bed, he subjected himself to all the blame in the world. He kept his head back to keep from crying. With his fists tightly closed, he hit his thighs with all the strength he had.

The silent treatment was initiated between Michael and his family after that. At suppertime, he refused to go downstairs, in spite of his father's repeated pleas. He threatened to send him back to his village, if he did not comply immediately. The words were far away and insignificant in Michael's ears. His mother loved the idea, shouting and swearing she could no longer suffer having this terrible child around. Somehow, Michael knew what was going on but kept from breaking down. He was calm. Not even the threats would make him change his mind. He was absolutely fed up. He prayed and prayed that they would turn their threats into action. This was his dearest dream: To leave and go far away from this unhappy place, to set foot again on familiar ground, to rediscover his beloved grandmother, his childhood friends, and enjoy life as he knew it. It seemed, so long ago.

He had had enough of the isolation, the cold, the snow, the ill-treatment. "You're from the jungle, Michael… You're stupid, Michael… You're a good-for-nothing." Leaving was the only soothing word he knew. Back home at least, he was Michael with an ounce of dignity. There, you are not judged by your shortcomings. The elders used to thank him and chant his name when he went to fetch their water. He had felt like a small prince.

What a beautiful life! Not at all like all the hell he'd been thrown into.

All that evening, a bad omen seemed to be permeating the house. Dinner was spent in a dismal, chilling atmosphere. Husband and wife seemed overwhelmed rather than angry. When they pointed their accusing finger at Michael, did they notice that their other three fingers were pointing back at them? Jennifer and Laura rested their spoons in the middle of their plates, and did not move an inch. Everyone's appetite had vanished regardless of the quality of the meal served. Angry, Florence got up, threw her napkin down on her chair and left. The father followed her a few minutes later. Jennifer and Laura cleared the table in silence.

Two weeks later, the father broke the news to the son. Michael ran to his room to celebrate. He had been waiting for this moment for quite some time now.

After living only nine months with his parents, Michael was forced to return home. The reasons were various: disobedience, laziness, bad behavior and much more, but for him, it was like a huge liberation. The truth of the matter was he was more than happy to leave. It didn't matter to him what his parents had said and done. What counted was that he was going back to a world made for him. This departure was the most wonderful thing to happen to him since the day he had received his backpack. He pulled the flight attendant by the hand, inviting her to rush. Surprised, his father and his wife watched. They were shocked to see Michael so cheerful about leaving. Laura kept waving her tiny little fingers in spite of her mother's attempts at stopping her. Little Laura insisted on waving goodbye to the only brother she knew. Michael looked towards his parents for one last time, but it was his young sister Laura he was really looking at. He flashed a final smile in her direction before disappearing behind the Customs restricted area.

The Village Boy

Michael's return home wasn't without noisy fanfare and under good guard. Grandmother sang, danced, and gratefully raised her arms to her good God, thanking him for bringing back her beloved grandson. The village was in joy. All the children had come to find out about the country of cold and snow. They touched Michael and felt him in an attempt to capture the feelings of his visit abroad. Michael was wild. He spread out his toys and told them about Belfast, but when he stated that the abroad that they imagined was the wrong place to be, the kids were enraged. They thought Michael was mocking them. Some bluntly got up and left. It didn't bother Michael. He meant what he said and no one could make him change his mind. In fact, he was very proud to say that life as it should be was here, in this village. A few zealous ones raised their voices and swore he was lying. Michael raised his voice, too. He did not like to be second guessed, when he was right. In the middle of this passionate debate, silence suddenly fell and everyone looked towards the main entrance. Michael wasn't following what was happening, so one of his cousins gave him a nudge to draw his attention.

Éliane had been standing still in the middle of the doorway.

One by one, the children moved out of the way, allowing her to come closer. She took a few steps forward before stopping a couple of meters away from him. Michael stood up to greet her. They looked into each other's eyes for what seemed to be an eternity. Automatically, Éliane took her friend Michael's hand and turned around. He dropped the toys he was holding and followed her willingly, a coy expression on his face as if to say, "Am I not right to come back?" They walked side-by-side, saying not a word with an inner peace that could not be disturbed.

This precious bond with the real world was reactivated. Michael joyfully and effortlessly got back to all of his old habits in every way. There was a lot of talk of how Michael's trip had produced a lot of changes in him, but Michael didn't think so.

At school, his new role of storyteller of elaborate journeys had made him a valued individual. As a student he even was doing great, too. Antima was proud of him when he brought home his report cards, semester after semester. To reward him, she never missed offering him barbecued chicken, something especially prepared just for him. Together with his friends, they would celebrate until well past his bedtime.

All was going well for Michael. He was happy with his simple life and newfound serenity with the village folk, all under the guidance of his beloved grandmother Antima.

Michael entered his twelfth year. Life was perfect until the day the big news broke.

It was Thursday, the school off day in the village. As usual, Michael had gone with his grandparents to the farm. It was drought season. The air was hot and dry. Michael's grandpa, sixty two years old, was worn out from years of hard farm work and could no longer keep up with the pace of his grandson. Every half hour, he would call for a much needed rest period to catch his breath. Michael would make sport of him. "You see, grandfather, I told you I would be stronger than you one day! I made twelve haystacks and you only made five!"

"My young one, this is the wearing down of time. A day will come when your own grandson will be saying the very same words to you."

"Not me! I will always be strong and in perfect shape."

"I said the same thing when I was your age. But here I am today, old and worn-out." With an air a little more serious,

Grandpa teased him. "Tell me, gladiator, when you become prime minister one day, in one of these big black fancy cars, I hope you will think of your poor old grandfather and grandma."

"Of course! When I am big, I will take grandmother and you with me to my house in the city."

"Oh, no. I don't want to live in one of these houses in the big city where toilets and kitchens are within the same walls. Those who live in big cities consider themselves to be more civilized people. I don't think so. All I want is to be buried in one of these glass coffins."

"But this is nothing, grandfather. If you want, I can even preserve your dead body for ever. That way, we can come visit you every Sunday after church. What do you think?"

"You little rascal! Wait until I catch you. I'll show you what I am made of. If you're waiting for me to die to play with my body," he said, as he started running after Michael.

Antima watched from under a palm tree, laughing. Grandpa was dodging in and out between the plants, trying to catch Michael, grumbling, "Where are you, you little rascal?...How many times have I told you: I don't want anyone to inject me with the poison we use to dry snakes up, hey?" Michael was having fun, playing hide-and-seek with his grandfather, who kept on calling him names, "You little brat. Wait till I catch you! You'll see!"

At the same time, a serious and excited voice called out to Michael, ending the game between him and his grandfather. The old man stopped, out of breath. Antima called from under the tree.

"Michael, it's your cousin. He has something important to tell you. Come out, now!"

Michael came out of his hiding place and shouted, "Koffi, what do you want? I'm in the middle of a game."

Koffi made his way through the plants and reached him, finally, out of breath.

"Your parents! Your parents!" he kept repeating.

"What?"

"Your parents! Your parents!"

"Say what you have to say!"

"Your mom and dad have arrived."

Without emotion, Michael said, "They've arrived and then what? Don't tell me that is why you almost broke your neck?"

"Your parents have come from abroad and that is all you find to say?"

"What do you want me to do… dance? I knew they were going to arrive today."

"You really don't know anything."

"No! You don't know anything. You should be watching where you walk instead. You're going to break the young plants."

Michael's grandfather was watching, but he pretended not to hear them.

This was irrelevant news to Michael's ears. There was one thing he did know, however: From now on, things would not be the same as before. For him, the good life was no more.

After spending two more days at the village, the time had come for Michael's father and his family to return to the capital city Accra where Anam had bought a house for his family in one of the posh districts of Accra. Michael didn't want to go, and he told them repeatedly, but no one would listen, not even Antima when it was stipulated it was a great opportunity for a better education. Michael went along once more, but this time came the breakdown of true order.

The feelings of Michael's departure were rather cold and cynical. All of his childhood friends were present to say goodbye. Éliane was waving her hand faithfully along with the rest of the village people. Although a little girl, her feminine instinct was telling her this separation would be permanent. Michael was following the whole scenario without any expression. Not a hint of emotion appeared on his face. Both father and mother kept exchanging looks. The attention displayed by the children towards Michael was surprising to them. Excited, Laura pulled Michael by the arm, away from his pals. She had a lot of things to tell him. Michael made an attempt to calm her, but she didn't want to listen to him. Jennifer hadn't paid any attention at all to the entire event since the beginning, very indifferent and not wanting to participate in any of it. Finally, Michael's father decided to start the car to Jennifer's great relief.

     Again, Michael was migrating to some unknown destiny, life he would prefer to be spared. Forever, precious ties were broken, putting an end to a wonderful past, a happy era and a sweet life. Michael was convinced his peaceful existence was being forever destroyed again. He made every desperate effort to hide his deep sorrow. His grandfather had always said, "Michael, a real man never shows his emotions. He must never cry on his own misery but fight for it. Tears are signs of weakness. When a man receives a call, he must not question the place it takes him to but just comply." Michael believed his grandparents and was in complete agreement with them, so he applied their lessons in this particular circumstance with utmost honor. His attitude was rather positive. Ever since the hour of departure had sounded, he was ready like a soldier at his first gathering under the flag.

The Ultimate Chaos

The atmosphere in the posh district was almost friendly in the next few days. Michael did his best to try to fit in, wanting as much as possible to make new friends. But these children were of another life. They were show-offs and arrogant. Their daily conduct differentiated them from his friends back in the village. He really didn't like those spoiled city kids, but still made an effort to conform because if he didn't, he would be left alone. After all, as a village child he possessed good manners that ran very deep. Nevertheless, adapting was difficult in the beginning, but when he finally understood their silly manners, he knew how to play their game, even better than they did. He actually found that they were not very profound in their way of seeing things. With the quick passing of time, Michael converted to his new life.

One month passed, then two. At the third month mark, the fragile, but progressing process of reconciliation between Michael and his parents collapsed like a house of cards. Things were no more like the early days. Now, even if the head dictated the daily activities, the heart didn't follow anymore. The friction between Michael and his parents was a rough road. The ultimate chaos had been reached. Time had come to play mind games. Here, each camp had to be true, worthy and most of all, the belligerents had to be well prepared to keep up with the new order.

Michael tried hard to fit his parent's design, but he always failed to adjust to their scale. One thing was sure, he was a village child and they just couldn't understand it. Above all, no matter how justified he was in his explanations, his arguments fell on deaf ears. Every single act, big or small, was a subject of contempt. As if by some dark magic, people could not look beyond his shortcomings. He was never made to feel he was a child like the others. Boundaries were outlined. He had to make sure he stayed in the place they had assigned to him, but where exactly? No one ever described it to him. Michael was labeled a mentally disabled child to justify themselves. He had to accept it, period. Moreover, he had to avoid seeking answers otherwise the anger would be unleashed onto him.

Days and nights, Michael endured and said nothing. It was the only way to look good in the eyes of the family. He struggled to survive the pains of repression and humiliation conferred upon him by his status. What status? The son of the famous surgeon raised in the deep end of the African forest? No one dared to tell him this either. Not one deed he accomplished around the house that brought him recognition. Anything having to do with him was subject to criticism. Disapproval and insults were his constant companions.

The only moments of peace he could manage to savor were during school classes, where he was always the first to arrive and the last to leave. So he spent most of this time daydreaming and thinking about what life would be like after school. The words of the teachers echoed far in his ears. Michael's teachers didn't understand why his school marks were not as good as those shown in his former report cards in the village. No one bothered to figure it out. In their eyes, he was like all those others of his kind - a feeble-minded and lazy kid who lacked nothing in his wealthy life, not caring about making a life of his own. After all, with parents like his, problems don't exist. This was the way people in town thought and there was nothing Michael could do about it.

His frustration grew as his school marks declined. This realization he noted with profound heartache. Night and day, in his dull moments, he thought of his grandmother. He could still hear her cheers over all the others, when he was named the first of his class. He could almost taste and smell the roasted chicken and all the trimmings of the feast that followed the ceremony. He could feel the love.

His beloved grandmother was always there for him, telling him stories like the one of 'Wansam' that she used to tell him to frighten him when he became too unruly. There was also 'Cigali,' goddess of speed, whom grandmother evoked at nighttime, when she wanted him to hurry up and go to the bathroom. "You have to hurry up, as the tale said. Otherwise you risk being taken away to the Kingdom of the Unknown." Michael had believed her stories firmly at first, but as he grew older, he understood it was just some trick she used to make him comply, though he continued to play the game. He promised himself he would tell her the truth the day she would come to see him. He imagined the expression on her face, when he would tell her, he knew that her stories of 'Wansam' and 'Cigali' were only jokes. She would try to catch him and squeeze his left cheek, but he will take off like a hare.

Amidst all of those thoughts, Michael started to laugh. He got up and filled a plastic bag with some personal belongings. The urge was there to flee through the woods, to run to the station, jump on a train, and go very far away where no one could find him, but he could never muster enough courage to follow through with it.

Michael was constantly thinking about his fate. He couldn't understand why or how he, the beloved grandson, came to be banished to the last echelon of humanity among his very own. What a bitter pill to swallow! Some days Michael tried to convince himself that he was truly responsible for all of his own misery. He tried some new strategies and worked like a housemaid, cleaning the house, washing the dishes, polishing the furniture, etc., but when they saw what he was doing, they just yelled at him to stop doing what the servants were paid to do. Quietly, he put down the broom, before they grabbed it out of his hands, and he went up to his room. There, he asked himself, "Why?" He held back and found comfort in an old, soothing memory, tucked away in a corner of his mind. This strategy was the only thing that had worked, since he came to live with his parents. He knew to keep his mouth shut and stay the farthest away from the other children. He knew not to contaminate them with his bizarre accent, his stupidity, his laziness, and all of the rubbish that he was so accused. He would be doomed if their perspective was not respected. From their point of view, every punishment was perceived as being good for him. When he had had enough of it, he raised his shoulders, as if to show them he could care less. But it was not true. Deep down, he was suffering even though he didn't want to show it.

    Sometimes, he would try to attract attention to himself by pushing them beyond their limits, hoping that they would send him home to his beloved grandma. He would break two or three plates of their dinner plates at a time, but contrary to his expectations. Only the same song was repeated over and over, "You're good for nothing. You are a complete failure. Why can't you be like your sisters?" When the floodgates opened, it was very difficult to stop the flow. Overwhelmed, Michael simply suffered.

    The ritual would resume as soon as his father came home from work, except this time, it would be as amplified as the punishment that went with it. Both parents, as if ceremonially, would order him to sit down again. They would cleanse him, wash him with bleach, dry him, and on an empty stomach, they would send him up to his room. It went on and on. Michael completely paralyzed by this infernal machine.

At school, he would manage to present his best behavior while still trying hard to live up to the condescending and mean treatment he was subjected to by some of the spoiled city kids. Michael was starting to feel the weight of all the misfortune on his frail shoulders. Even the expression on his face was beginning to speak volumes. He was trying so hard to appear to be a normal teenager but the emotions he had managed to control inside of him were now too strong....They were finding their way out. Michael had had enough.

One evening, the teasing escalated into a fistfight with one of his classmates. This bully, trying to make Michael look bad, yelled out, "Look at you, idiot. Look at your life. Don't you see that this woman treats you like a dog? She is not your mother, don't you know that?"

The words sounded very distant and bizarre to Michael. He had heard very clearly what the other kid had said, but he wasn't sure if it was really directed to him. Michael asked him, "Are you referring to me?" He needed to make sure he hadn't misunderstood. The troublemaker, proud, restated the hurtful phrase in a loud voice so everyone could hear. It was unmistakable. Michael was convinced and they went at it.

Michael set free his opponent who lay powerless on the ground, while his mouth kept spewing venom. He didn't want to hear any more. Dragging behind him the unending chain of insults, he ran home to announce the shocking news to his father. Breathless, he threw himself at his feet. He demanded to know the truth, the whole truth, and immediately. Michael felt as though he was suddenly in a position of power. His question was clear and simple, "Dad, is it true that this woman is not my mother?"

His father's heart sank deeper in his chest. He was searching for the right thing to say to Michael, but couldn't find anything. Crying with anger, Michael shouted again, "Is it true that she is not my mother?" Anam shook his head affirmatively. He opened his mouth to provide an explanation, but Michael didn't want to know any more than he did. He knew enough. His father tried to hold him back, but Michael freed himself with force. War was now declared. Father and son were entering into a permanent conflict; one they would never dare admit to. The chain that connected the family structure was crumbling before their eyes. Anam remained standing in the middle of the room. After a long silence, he headed for the nearest cabinet. He took out a bottle of whisky and poured himself a glass, then a second, then a third.

  Michael was on the run through the streets. He had no exact destination in mind but he kept going. He ran, walked, stopped, and started running again. So many questions were invading his mind. At least he understood why she was always so mean towards him during those years. He knew something in the mother and son bond was missing somewhere, but he could never figure it out. Now he understood. Even if he wasn't getting any closer to understanding and explaining everything that was happening to him, he at least had a clue. Michael tried to identify a reason, but he felt so empty he could no longer focus on logic. He wandered till nightfall. He joined the street kids in an abandoned building downtown for the night, one very hellish night.

  Strangely, his family was happy, when he walked into the house the next day, after police had found him. He knew their language already and he didn't want to fall into the trap. The boundaries were set and he wanted to stick to them forever. He spoke to no one, went up to his room and locked his door.

The Defense Instinct

Another year went by, Michael was now thirteen years old. Territories clearly branded with the marks of each group. Everyone had to stay within his own boundary lines. Michael did his best to be very obedient to the rules. Unfortunately, in this war of nerves he was the weakest link. Still, Michael didn't want to give up an inch of his turf. On the contrary, he was ready to defend himself, and best of all, he did not have to behave as one of them. Now that he knew he had no mother in the picture. The atmosphere was oppressive to live in, but Michael was prepared to adjust and hold up against it.

One evening at suppertime, the dose of unfairness was a little too strong for Michael, and unable to contain his anger, he flew into a rage when his so-called mother called him good for nothing. Enough was enough. Michael rose, pulled the tablecloth off the table and hammered his fist on the surface. Food spilled everywhere and dishes went crashing to the floor. His stepmother was visibly shaken, Laura and Jennifer were frightened, and his father watched without losing his composure. Michael took a deep breath, stood up firmly, and stormed out of the house. His breaking point was reached. A new beginning was set. His days of crying and feeling sorry for himself were over. It was as if he were climbing a step higher in his manhood. He was taking charge of himself, like an orphan. The village people always said that for an orphan, living is like stepping into the jungle. From now on, Michael refused to submit for anyone's favor. He no longer operated under the old rules. He had his own plans for the future and could not care less about what his stepmother or his father thought. The only thing he knew was that he had to accept things as they were. Isn't that how life is supposed to be after all?

One thing was sure in his mind: His future was in his own hands, and nowhere else. He would never depend on anybody from that moment on. That became his personal commitment.

Every day after class, he wandered in the neighborhood without knowing where he was going, and each day he would go further and deeper into the heart of the city. One foggy afternoon, he had been walking on the east side for only a few minutes, when he heard screaming. He quietly headed in that direction. Michael was mesmerized by what he saw. A karate training camp set amid the bushes with a real Chinese master, like he'd only seen in movies. What a discovery! Since then, that location became his promised land. Not one evening did he miss honoring that place with his presence. Every day after school, he would disappear for the remainder of the evening. Michael's days now had a meaning as he watched the young men and women in white kimonos, striped by different color belts. He particularly admired the teacher, Chan, a middle-aged Asian man, small but muscular, standing in front of the students, always trying to get the best from them.

One particular evening, burrowed in his small hiding place, he was admiring the prowess of the fighters when someone pulled him out of his station. He was dragged by his belt to the middle of the battlefield.

With a funny accent, the trainer announced, mockingly, "There is a spy among us. I have been alerted to his presence for the past couple of days....Who are you working for, young man?" Michael wasn't sure what the man was insinuating by that. Michael extended his hand to introduce himself, "I am Michael Deh. I want to learn karate."

With a snicker, the man shouted to his students, "Did you hear that? He wants to learn karate."

Everybody burst out laughing. The master went up into the ring and invited Michael to do the same. With no hesitation,

Michael followed suit. The man assumed a fighting position and asked Michael to punch him in the stomach, which Michael did, even before he was given the signal. The man tottered backwards and almost fell. Everyone laughed again. Michael was proud of his accomplishment. The master was not too happy, but he was impressed nonetheless. He invited Michael into the club.

"Little monster! You are now a member of the team."

Michael jumped to touch the sky, landed on his two legs again, dropped down, and started to roll on the ground. They all watched him in amazement. The dream that he had was actually happening. He couldn't believe his ears. In all the confusion and excitement, he almost tried to kiss master Chan, but stopped himself in good time.

After listening to the instructions, the schedule, and uniform requirements, Michael ran home to his father and to ask for his support. It was the first time he really asked for something. His father didn't hesitate. It was a rather good opportunity to take up again with the son gone astray. Michael was devoting himself seriously to his new pastime. The following days, he transformed his bedroom into a second training facility. At home and at the training camp, Michael worked hard to get ahead. He was a good student and his master was quite impressed with his performance.

After only three months, Michael was promoted to the rank of yellow belt, something that had never happened before at that particular arena. Michael kept climbing the ladder, relentlessly and without obstacles. His physical endurance and his performance dazzled everybody. He was an exemplary student.

After one year of training, his master decided to have him compete for the Tae-Kwon Do National junior championship. His father was not very happy with the news, but Michael didn't want to lose the opportunity. He didn't care about what everybody else thought, but he really wanted was his father's blessing. His grandmother had always said that it was very important in life to have the blessing of your parents when you want to do something. After a few days of threatening not to return to school, he finally received his father's permission. The rest was of absolutely no importance to him.

    The anticipated day had finally arrived. Competitors had come from all over the country. Excitement was in the air. All sorts of intimidating mind games were at play. Michael was fully aware of them and he remained undisturbed. He was exuding a natural confidence and a serene calmness. He looked like someone who knew what place he'd take and he was ready for it. If only his grandmother could be there to cheer for him like the old times, but no matter what, Antima would be the first person he would announce the good news to. Everyone could cheer and celebrate, but only with his grandma could the real glory be obtained.

    The selection period had begun on a cheerful and festive note. Michael went through the matches without real effort. At the end of four fights, which he won with the upper hand, he reached the quarterfinals, then the semi-finals. His opponent was a tough guy. At sixteen years old, he had already been national champion twice. Michael was only fourteen years old and it was his first fight outside of the Dojo. Nevertheless, he wasn't worried at all. His master was praising and encouraging him. He massaged his shoulders and told him he was capable of winning.

    The whistle sounded a few minutes later. His master whispered one final instruction into his ear. The two potential finalists stood in the middle of the ring. They listened to the rules then acknowledged the official and the referee with a bow. They had just barely bowed to one another when Michael spun himself around and swept the legs out from under his opponent, who fell flat on his stomach. The crowd rose in astonishment. The room was still. The referee counted to ten. The young man couldn't get up. A technical knockout!

The crowd gave Michael a standing ovation. They sang and chanted his name loudly. His master lifted him up off the ground. The room was in total euphoria but Michael was indifferent. He had not completed his mission yet. The final was what counted the most in his eyes. He waited impassively, observing the fighting technique of his upcoming opponent.

"It is a good sign," whispered his master. "He will be exhausted and you will take him quickly."

The officials stopped the fight at the end of regulation time, thirty minutes later. The opponents with the most points were designated to move onto the final battle. It was the moment that had been long awaited. The two fighters studied each other. The opponent, who had watched some of Michael's early matches, was jumping at his slightest motions. The crowd was very amused and laughed. After several minutes of observation, Michael decided to enter into his challenger's game. He began a sweeping movement, but was blocked immediately. His opponent kept jumping up and down like a grasshopper. The crowd was hysterical; the scene so hilarious. Michael made it last for a few minutes more, and then he changed his tactics. He executed a great sitting flip, but instead of aiming at the legs, he delivered a powerful blow to the left cheek of his opponent. He fell over on his nape. He stood up again, trying to figure out exactly what had happened to him. The crowd shouted, "Mike! Mike! Mike!"

The two stars assumed their combat position again. They looked at each other, studying one another for a few minutes, before engaging in battle again. This time, the blows were methodical and calculated. The desire of each opponent to win had reached a high. It was the dream of every finalist. All the intentions are worth it, but the most important thing is to succeed in reaching the goal of one's aspiration. Michael thought of his grandmother and her advice regarding will power. He smiled.

Minutes went by. Both rivals were still equal after a long spirited fight. Then Michael stopped fighting. The crowd stood in astonishment. Chan screamed at Michael to go forward, wiggling his hands in his face. Michael stood very still. His opponent gestured to provoke him for a fight, but Michael did not respond. No one knew what was going on in his head, except Michael himself. Suddenly, his mind frozen on an episode of his life as his stepmother was wiggling her hands in his face, yelling, "Michael, you are good for nothing....You're a little bastard.Your life will be nothing but a failure....You're a bum!"

The crowd waited, immobile and silent. Some started to boo. Michael didn't move an inch. His opponent kept urging him to come on, but he still wouldn't move. Confused, he too, stood there motionless. Suddenly, Michael shook his head as if he was awaking from a nightmare. His eyes were blood red. A spasm of anger crossed his face. He let out a ferocious battle cry, startling the officials and the crowd. In an indescribable rage, he darted straight towards his opponent with such aggression that his opponent ran out of the ring.

The crowd went wild. The referee gave the young man a first warning, then a second one. On the third time, he came back to the ring. Everyone could see that he was visibly shaken, even though he managed to control himself. Michael jumped his opponent, and gave him a beating with punches and kicks of such furry, the young man ran away from the ring again, losing by disqualification. Michael was the indisputable winner. Everyone, including the officials, was laughing. The atmosphere was that of a circus. Michael had become a new hero: The fighter every adversary flees. The following day, his name made the headlines in the national daily newspaper, which praised his unique fighting method. Michael Deh was placed on a pedestal in the martial arts arena of the West African country.

The years passed. The name Michael Deh was on every lip and every conversation. Wherever he walked, there was always a crowd behind him. There was not a child in the country that did not dream of one day becoming just like him. He was endlessly collecting cups and titles. He had become the most dreaded adversary in his category.

Aside from his athletic life, he clung to his studies more seriously. Sometimes, he would ask himself whether he was simply doing really well or whether he was being favored because of his reputation. To him, the choice was clear; studies came second. This was a sore point between him and his father. Michael's father insisted that his future belonged solely in his studies, but Michael would bring his fist down on the table and maintain that his future was where he was receiving recognition right now. Michael was himself only when he was in a ring or at a competition. There, he was a man everyone respected: a champion. He felt real and worthy. It was the only place where he really lived.

In the end, Michael received his high school diploma. He did it for his grandmother. He never wanted the sacrifices she made in his early school days to be squandered. To all those children who idolized him, he wanted to say that sports are important, but studies mattered a great deal as well. There was a certain personal pride in proving that he was not "Michael, the fool," Now, he could lead his life as he wanted. He trusted his strength. Strength was the only thing he could depend on and he was convinced it would take him very far in life. No one was ready to challenge him on that, unless they were ready for a fight. Challengers bizarrely became a rare breed in the country.

Michael's father and stepmother were far from convinced that his future was guaranteed, in spite of his determination and the evidence of his success. His stepmother, in particular, was convinced that he was still nothing, but a brawler. Even if he did fight wearing a special uniform with a meaningful belt, she thought he would revert back to the street environment naturally suited to people like him and end up in jail. Both parents believed that the articles written about Michael in the newspapers were as ephemeral as the paper they were printed on. They were categorical on their position and were not the least bit impressed. Michael knew what they were thinking about him, but he didn't care. He had found his path and he wanted follow it to the end. He was confident they would have a change of heart the day he won the nation's big cup. They would all have to shut their mouths. But for now, neither he nor his parents were having the last word, and only the fruit of his labor would convince them.

One day, when he was getting ready to leave the house for his practice, his father surprised him with his suggestion to sign Michael up for driving lessons. He thought to himself, "Finally! My father and I can have some normal interaction. I'll be just like the other children in the neighborhood. How wonderful!" He was happy and eager to find out whether his father was sincere or not. He knew him too well. He never made a decision arbitrarily – he always had something else in mind, a second agenda. He knew his father's favors were always calculated and were never priceless.

Michael's father had gone up to his room, shortly after their conversation. Michael waited a few minutes, then followed. He put his ear to the door and listened as the husband reported to his wife. She was shouting, yelling, and obviously angry, "How dare you wanting to pay for this hooligan to learn how to drive?"

With a calmness a player uses only when he is sure to checkmate, he said, "Don't you understand?"

"What is there to understand?" she asked.

"Look. With all those cups and titles he keeps winning, the newspaper coverage and everything else… all this can go to a teenager's head. One day, he may feel like stealing a car to go joyriding with his friends and, without a driver's license, you know the damage this could cause! I want him to know how to drive. This way, if he decides to steal one of our cars, we stand a better chance of recovering it intact." She laughed and with all the tenderness in the world, she congratulated him for having had such an ingenious idea. She added, somewhat to apologize for her outburst, "All I needed was an explanation from you."

"Now that you have it, what do you think?"

"You are the best husband a woman could ever dream of. You own my heart." They both went on with long bouts of laughter.

Michael was furious! He tightened his fists, but he didn't say anything. Quietly, he placed the money and the booklets his father had given him by the door and ran off. The noise attracted the attention of his father who immediately came out of his room, but Michael was already long gone. His father's repeated calls weren't enough to stop him.

A few years went by and Michael kept his winning streak. He had finally turned eighteen and approached the national senior championship; the championship he had long awaited. His sponsors had decided to offer him a stay at the Mafou hotel, the most impressive hotel in the country.

A young woman, Sabine, worked at the hotel as the service coordinator. At thirty years old, Sabine still looked young and very beautiful. Her dark, smooth complexion was radiant with a nose finely chiseled, a lovely face, and a splendid neckline. She had everything that could induce men into infatuation, including a pubescent teenager like Michael.

When their eyes met, Michael's heart started pounding. It was love at first sight. Michael had never had such feelings before, and they were far better than the anger and sparse joy related to his victories. Sabine was thunderstruck by this teenager's gaze. She was familiar with how men looked at her, but she truly felt there was something special in the eyes of this young man. Sabine had grown indifferent to the many wandering eyes since she started working at the hotel, but she never let them bother her. In choosing this profession, she knew she had to be cautious with men. In spite of the numerous proposals, she was still unattached since her divorce two years ago. She wanted to be patient, to have an open mind, and to not rush into another relationship, like she had done in the past.

As she smiled back at Michael, she felt a little embarrassed at being the subject of attention to this nervous teenager. His mind was racing with all the things his friends had told him about love. Something had taken root in him. He did not know what to call it, but he felt he wasn't the same person anymore. He wanted to confide in her all his pains and joys, tell her everything, dedicate this fight to her, and his entire life.

She checked him in, called another lady to fill for her, and escorted them to a separate compound and returned to her post. Michael couldn't concentrate anymore. His instructor tried very hard to bring Michael back to reality, but Michael's mind appeared too far-gone. He was no longer listening, even when his instructor was madly insisting that the game plan for winning big fights lay in the single life. As soon as Chan turned his back, Michael ran straight to Sabine's workplace. He waited behind the building until she got off work. Since then, together every night, they would take off for another adventure around town. Neither the advice of his instructor, nor the warnings of his sponsors, could stop him.

With Sabine, Michael was a free spirit. He could talk about anything and everything: his childhood with his grandma, his relation with his father, his stepmother, and the rest. She listened quietly with interest. When he finished, she told him he was not at all like his parents thought he was. They laughed together and never got tired of each other's company. He could not help but to invite her to the final. Sabine said yes. He was overjoyed. His dearest grandma could not be there, but Sabine would be the first most important person watching him fight for the first time. She was to occupy the place of honor, at the first row. Michael felt as though he could move mountains. Strangely, he knew that only the intense closeness between him and Sabine had become his reason to live now. He felt like a totally new person. When he found himself alone in his room, he would shout for joy and throw himself on his bed to jubilate.

It was four o'clock on competition day. The arena was packed to capacity. Most of the spectators had come to see Michael. Sabine was sitting in the first row as promised. The tension was increasing in the dressing room. Michael was sitting on the ground, concentrating. He always does this before a fight. The pressure was enormous. He must not only demonstrate that he is a champion of all categories, but of all occasions. Most of all, Sabine was in the audience.

A few minutes before the fight, Sabine decided to go wish him luck one last time, but the promoters in the front row tried to keep her away. When Michael realized what was going on, he ordered them to let her in. His instructor wanted to intervene, but Michael's body language told him he'd better not bother. He stood up as she walked towards him, and took her by the hand. They smiled and went towards the back of the room. They stopped. She whispered something in his ear, then she kissed him before running out of the room. He watched for a brief moment. A huge smile lit up his face.

It was time for the opening ceremony. First came the introduction speech, followed by a presentation of the opponents. Finally, the signal was given for the fights to begin. No one was ready to give in. The competitors even seemed a little more serious than usual. Michael looked as if he were injected with a serum of invincibility. Sabine watched amazed. The eliminating matches were for him a mere warm-up exercise. His powerful kicks and punches were sending his competitors into the abyss, one by one. He kept up this pace until the final match.

This time his opponent was of a larger size. He was nicknamed "The Executioner" because of his brutal and violent methods. He was also the Defense Minister's personal bodyguard. All the spectators were standing. Michael looked in Sabine's direction. She winked and waved with her right hand. He felt more confident than ever.

The referee gave his signal. Michael's opponent delivered a steady flow of direct kicks and Michael was able to deflect them. He was in no hurry to counter-attack and the crowd became agitated and started screaming for Michael to do something, "Go Michael! Demolish him!" Michael could hear them, but was in no rush to strike back. This calm, which characterizes every great champion, gave him control of the situation. He waited for the perfect moment, then sent a direct kick to the chest of his opponent. The man staggered backwards a few steps and the crowd started to cheer, "Michael! Michael! Michael!"

This was the moment he had been waiting for. He delivered two other good kicks to the stomach of his rival, who writhed in pain. The referee stopped the fight for a few seconds, then allowed it to resume. The crowd was chanting louder, "Michael Deh! Michael Deh!"

The two men took their fighting positions once again. The fight was now taken to a new level. Each contender looked for the right opportunity to deliver the final blow. Michael delivered quick hits and retreated back. He didn't throw his kicks at random. Every move he made was calculated. His opponent tried hard with violent moves, but he could not reach Michael. Towards the end of the second round, Michael moved as if he was walking away. His opponent rushed after him carelessly, and at that exact moment, Michael turned and sent his adversary to the mat with a powerful kick in the stomach. The Executioner fell backward. He stood up, but fell again once more. The referee motioned for the doctors to step in. The diagnosis was clear. The man had two broken ribs. The referee blew his whistle indicating the end of the fight. Michael was proclaimed champion. A roar of applause and cheers irrupted in the arena.   Once again, Michael had demonstrated that he was the master of Tae-Kwon Do in this country. There was no doubt about it: Michael was Ghana's strongest man. Sabine made her way through the crowd that had converged around Michael. When she finally made her way through to the champion, she threw her arms around him and showered him with kisses. Ecstatic, he lifted her up off the ground as she screamed in joy. The pact between Michael and Sabine was sealed forever so they thought.

   That evening, Sabine organized a big celebration party in her apartment. Michael was a new man, a happy man. All night, Michael couldn't stop talking. Sabine listened and kept complimenting him, calling him her champion. Michael's instructor took him aside and asked, "What did she whisper to you before the fight?"

   "She said, 'Okay.'"

Amused, his master gave him a pat on the back and jokingly said, "You are lucky. Go, and enjoy life!"

It was a perfect evening. The guests were drinking, eating, and having fun. At two o'clock in the morning, one of them asked if Michael could give him a ride back home. Michael delegated the task to one of his cousins, but the guest refused. He wanted Michael and nobody else. He persisted enough until Michael decided to give him a ride on his motorcycle.

On his way back, Michael sensed he was being followed, but he paid little attention. A driver in a black Toyota kept flashing his lights at him, but Michael kept going. Suddenly, in his side mirror, he could see that the car was quickly approaching. Now it was obvious, he was being followed. He wasn't sure what to do. He held on to his handlebars tightly, distributed his weight perfectly on his motorcycle, and prepared to go full throttle. Then he felt a big jolt. The car had hit him from behind. Michael's motorcycle spun around. He wondered why someone would want to hurt him or kill him. Who was it? Why? Michael and the other driver were stopped. Michael was facing the car, Next to the driver, sat the man he had beaten in the finals, Even from a distance, Michael could sense the hatred oozing out of him. In the back seat, four big men were laughing. The Executioner had a cynical smile on his face. For a moment Michael thought of fighting them off, but when the man pointed a gun at him, Michael understood fleeing was the only solution. He quickly spun his motorcycle around, gave the throttle a single twist as far as it could turn, and before his attackers realized what he was doing, Michael had disappeared down the road. The assailants sped after him as fast as they could, but it was too late to catch up with him Out of breath, Michael returned and joined the party. He summoned Sabine into her room to tell her what had happened. She insisted he call the police, but Michael refused. The party continued until the wee hours of the morning and without any additional mishaps.

A new life had begun for Michael. The partnership between him and Sabine was evolving nicely. He was savoring the flavor of true friendship, as Sabine was genuine and sincere. For Michael, she had become a lover, a friend, and an ally. She was everything he needed to make him an accomplished man. For the most part, Sabine's place had become home for Michael. He stayed there more than anywhere else. Together, they created new career plans. She said all the publicity he was receiving gave him the ticket to success. He agreed. Soon, he was wearing three-piece suits more often than his Tae-Kwon Do uniform. Michael got used to his new lifestyle rather quickly. So many doors were opening for him. The business world welcomed him with enthusiasm, and like a chameleon, he blended into his new surroundings marvelously.

The Loyalty

Michael and Sabine entered forever into an intimate commitment. There was never any decision one made without the other. One evening, they were having dinner when Sabine suggested to Michael that buying a house would be a good investment for him. He found the idea brilliant. Michael was apparently eager to say yes to everything Sabine proposed. He felt she had his best interests at heart, after all, and she was the only one who truly loved him beside Antima. He wanted to enjoy this feeling forever.

Michael welcomed the idea of accumulating wealth. He thought that gaining worldly treasures might help him lose some of the awful memories that were so hard to forget. After all, buying a house at eighteen could be what he needed to win the esteem of his parents. Michael was ready to do anything just to have his parents on his side.

The day had come. After visiting four or five houses, they found a small charming villa on the seashore. Sabine immediately fell in love with it, "This one! You must buy this one." Michael smiled and shook the agent's hand. Beaming, Sabine jumped and wrapped her arms around Michael's neck, "I am so proud of you!" He signed the contract and the house was his. At eighteen, Michael was already owner of a house; something not very common in his country. Very soon, the news reached every corner of the country. Michael was put on an even higher pedestal. A few days later, he was granted the import-export license, an important document previously granted only to the country's elites. Michael was now part of high society.

Besides Michael's success and achievements in the business world, he kept winning in the athletic arena. Michael was a success as a sportsman and businessman. As more and more opportunities were presented, Michael continued to set higher goals for himself. One of which was the Olympics, but for that he needed higher athletic and physical training, and that would mean going abroad. Also, the thought of his birth mother had been increasingly present in his mind the past few years and he wanted to know who she was. Michael decided to leave for a different adventure.

One day in July 1985, Michael invited his father and his grandmother over to his house to let them know of his plans. The news took his father by surprise. His fingers, weakened by the alcohol, shook and played with the buttons of his shirt, unable to find a resting place. His grandmother held her head between her hands. Her eyes set on a corner of the carpet. An eternity of silence went by. Then, Antima reached into her handbag and withdrew a passport and a birth certificate folded many times over, "You will need these."

Without hesitation, Michael reached out for the papers and took them. He looked them over and over, in silence. Hearing of his Canadian citizenship by birth was a new mystery, another puzzle, but he dared not to ask. Uncomfortable and confused, his father promised to help locate Michael's mother for him. Michael thanked him. Then, after a few moments, his father added, "It's a long story. It is best if your mother tells it to you herself some day." He took his wallet out of his pocket and retrieved a picture of her. He handed it to Michael, "She's an extraordinary woman. You'll have the opportunity to know her better than I did."

Michael glanced at his grandmother then looked at his father again before he grabbed the picture. He studied it for a long time, and then in a desolate voice said, "I hope to find out the entire truth."

His grandmother tried to change the subject, "Oh, I almost forgot! Eliane has many things to tell you. She told me that you stopped writing her. This is not nice on your part, you know. She speaks so well of you."

Michael wanted to say something but the main door entrance bell rang. It was Sabine. She entered. Michael's father and grandmother exchanged looks. Antima glanced at Sabine and then at Michael. He jumped at the opportunity to introduce Sabine to his family.

"Sabine, this is my father and this is my grandmother."

"It is a real pleasure to meet you, Antima! Michael always speaks to me about you."

Antima looked past Sabine as if what she said hadn't been addressed to her. Sabine understood she was not welcome. She was experienced enough to know about in-laws. She sought a way out. "Mike, I think I'll wait outside if you don't mind."

"No, we were just about to finish. My father was leaving, but Antima is staying with us. We are taking her out for dinner tonight."

In her native language, Antima spoke suddenly and vehemently. "You won't see me at the restaurant with this little witch. You had taste when you were younger, but now you don't! No, thank you. I'm going back home. There's a nice plate of kinké just waiting for me."

Antima got up, took her handbag and followed her son. Sabine asked Michael what his grandmother had said, but Michael said it was nothing she should be worried about. Sabine knew he wasn't telling the truth. Antima stepped into her son's car, sneering at Sabine with disgust. She didn't even respond to Michael and Sabine's farewell.

Sabine explained to Michael that all grandmothers are alike and that he shouldn't worry. They made light of it and returned to the house. It was time for dinner. The houseboy had already served their cocktail. Michael drank it in one shot. His mind was elsewhere. He wanted to share this moment with his grandma. He knew one thing for sure: Nothing could ever break the bond between his grandma and her beloved grandson. Nevertheless, a decision had to be made.

The Reunion

Three months went by. Michael finally decided to board the plane for Canada. His grandmother, Sabine and all other family members were at the airport, except for his stepmother and her two girls. Her argument was she didn't feel well.

Everybody was waving incessantly. Michael looked and smiled at everyone on his path, unable to contain his joy as he stepped on the plane. He sat next to a man of about forty. They exchanged greetings, then nothing. Michael remained pensive in his seat. To pass the time, he took a book out of his bag and started to read. The engine roared to announce their departure. Michael glanced a last look outside, but nobody was in sight. He crossed his chest, tensed up, and quickly fastened his seat belt. Deep inside, he swore he would never get on a plane again as a strange fear fell over him. All of the security and emergency procedures explained by the flight attendants meant nothing to him. All he wanted was for them to let him sleep. He let out a sigh of relief when their recital finally ended. After the eight-hour flight and one stopover in Madrid, Michael finally touched the ground of his birthplace. What a strange sensation!

Michael found a room at the City Home, 427 Parliament Street. The building was old and dark but the room was comfortable. A wonderful feeling came over him, the kind you have when you really feel at home somewhere. He was proud and happy to have successfully accomplished the first phase of his journey abroad with a roof over his head. The second phase would be getting a telephone line to connect with the world and particularly with his mother.

Michael was about to hear from the woman who had conceived him, the woman who, as far as he knew, had shipped him out as a 'Diplomatic Package' a while ago. On the contrary, he had no more anger, only more questions. But for those questions to be answered, he would have to wait another three days. That was the closest appointment for the phone service.

Michael wanted to just meet her. Period! As for the many questions he had, he wondered, if they were really worth the pain of asking. He pondered the past over and over in his mind. He just couldn't understand his mother's motive. He painfully recalled how she had never written to him in twenty years. Not even a postcard. It would have been a simple matter of a few words and a stamp. Michael would have been so happy; he would have kept it in his bag, always. When people say there is nothing as strong as a mother's love, he had to disagree. For him, this statement was far from the truth. He didn't believe maternal love was a natural instinct. His young mind told him that such love is not inbred, but rather cultivated. Michael took another look at himself. Did he really know enough about his mother to pass judgment? He really didn't care about the major issues of her past. He had made a success of his life despite his mother's absence. That is what mattered. And it was thanks to Antima. But at that point he wanted to see his mother to find out where he came from, to determine the origin of his character. Would he be more like her, or more like his father? He had a splendid picture of her, but pictures don't always tell the truth. He had to see her in the flesh. Finally. How exciting it will be!

It was ten o'clock in the morning, when the phone company technician rang the doorbell. Michael jumped the stairs four steps at a time trying to get to him as fast as possible. He opened the door. They exchanged a handshake and the man followed him in. He started to work spreading his tools out on the bed, after asking Michael if it bothered him. The technician didn't look up at him anymore. He pulled some wires, cut them, attached them together, and, after a long period of silence, he asked, "Are you really African?"

"Yes. Why?"

"Well," said the man. "Africans I know are black. You must be from South Africa," he continued, without giving Michael a chance to speak, "They say that over there blacks and whites don't mix. Is this true?"

"Yes, but this will all end one day."

"You're very optimistic, young man. That's what it takes to succeed in this county, but a lot of people just don't get it. In my opinion, that's the way everyone should be - optimistic."

The discussion continued as the man continued fighting with the various wires. Ten minutes later, he plugged the telephone in, dialed a number and said a few words before hanging up. He came back to Michael, proudly. "You're now in wonderland. Here, without a telephone, life sucks."

Michael wasn't listening to the man talking anymore. All he wanted at this precise moment was to pick up the phone, dial a particular number, and wait. They shook hands and said goodbye.

Michael pounced on the telephone and dialed. The phone rang and rang. Then the voice of a little girl came on the fourth ring. Michael asked to speak to her mother. She asked him to wait, then she shouted at the top of her lungs, "Mom, it's for you. It's a gentleman."

"Tell him to hold on for a few seconds. I'll be right there."

The little girl relayed the message, and then put the receiver down. Michael waited a few moments before hearing a voice at the other end.

"Hello?"

"Hi. This is Michael," he said with his voice cracking. "I arrived a week ago and my father gave me your number… I'm calling to say hello."

"What is your name, again?"

"Michael… Michael Deh… Michael Deh Anam."

Silence reigned. The woman held her breath for an eternity, and returned on the speaker with cracking voice, "Mikey, give me your number. I will call you back in a minute."

He gave her his number and they both hung up at the same time. The mother staggered and let herself fall into an armchair, dizzy. Her memory was taking her back twenty years ago. She was reliving the embassy episode with Michael smiling in his cradle. She shook her head in an attempt to dispel the memories, but the images were frozen.

Patricia, 8 years old, ran in, bombarding her with countless questions. The mother's answers were faraway and incoherent. Visibly shaken, she got up, tightened her fists, held her head, started to pace, returned to sit, and dropped down into the chair. She didn't know what to hold onto. Patricia watched, dumfounded. She gestured for help. Mother shook her head fiercely. No! Trying to help anyone in such circumstances was practically mission impossible. The little girl screamed for help. Her big brother, Joe, thirteen, rushed in as the kids gathered around their mother. The task was a difficult one. After a few minutes, the mother broke down into a shivering and sobbing state. She held on to the armchair and let it all out.

On his side, Michael remained perplexed. He asked himself whether unearthing the past had been a good decision on his part. If not, it would turn out to be a terrible mistake. He would be rejected again, twenty years after being cast aside the first time. He was turning every bit of the past over in his head trying to hold onto a piece of memory that could have provoked the anger that made her send him away. Unfortunately, he was confronted to the limit of childhood memory lane. There was no episode of his childhood worth justifying what she has done to him. Michael couldn't explain the injustice that had victimized him since birth. The vision of his stepmother when he was nine years old still haunted his day and night. She had been very rude to him, calling him all sorts of names. But isn't being treated this way by a stepmother normal when your own mother has deserted you? Perhaps he was just a miserable child after all. Maybe she had a good reason.

Michael's mind was wondering when the phone rang. He picked it up immediately. It was his mother.

"Hello! Michael?"

"Yes?"

"I would like… Hey… Could you come to the house? Is this possible?"

"When?"

"Tonight at seven o'clock. That way, we could have supper together. Let me give you the address."

In a shaky voice, she carefully spelled out the address, making sure she didn't make any mistakes. Michael wrote the address in his notebook. Once again, they hung up nearly at the same time.

It was seven o'clock. The entire family was at the table: the mother, the oldest son and the daughter. The husband was not there; he died of cancer six years earlier. The family still mourned him but life was going on.

A heavy silence reigned in the dining room. The trio son, daughter and mother were glancing at each other, occasionally diverting their eyes towards the door.

Michael was fifteen minutes late. He was at the front door of 2431 Rue des Damnés, but hesitated to press the doorbell. Finally he did it. Joe was the first one to jump up and run to open the door. Joe was white and Michael mixed. The two brothers looked at each other. They didn't know whether they should embrace or not. A few seconds later, Joe asked, "Are you Michael?"

"Yes," Michael answered.

"I'm Joe. Come on in!"

Everybody stood around the table. Mother and son looked at each other. There were no obvious signs of emotion. Michael felt neither hot nor cold. His mother was standing in front of him for the first time in twenty years but he wasn't feeling anything in particular. He walked towards her and extended his hand automatically. His mother did the same. Michael then turned to Patricia and greeted her in the same fashion. The welcoming formality completed, Joe invited Michael to sit down.

Reunited for the first time, mother and son studied each other like two strangers. The mother was visibly uneasy, although she did try to appear controlled and relaxed. Dinner was spent in a pleasant atmosphere though, neither joyful nor sad.

It was nine o'clock when Michael decided to leave. "Can I talk to you?" asked his mother. Michael said yes without hesitation. She pulled him aside in a separate room and tried to collect her thoughts. "I don't even know how to begin." She explained nervously." "I don't need to know." Michael said instantly. "Please, let me explain." She tried again. "No!" insisted Michael. She got it. Michael refused to go down the memory lane. She didn't want it either. Mother and son stood still. An eternity passed. They returned to the dinning room. Michael was rather cheerful. He said goodbye and was already at the door. His mother kept repeating that her door was always open to him, and Michael kept repeating: "Okay! Okay! Okay!"

They hugged and Michael left. On the way home, he decided to take a long walk. The streets were crowded. Michael mingled into the crowd. Half an hour later, he stopped at a café where the chairs were set up on the sidewalk. He sat down but didn't order anything. Five to ten minutes went by. He stood up and went on his way. A few steps away, the sirens of a police car tore through the air. Some gunshots followed. The peaceful street suddenly turned into panic. Crowds were running everywhere. Michael started to run. Instead of following the crowd, he had joined a group of kids who had veered into a maze of alleys. He ran so fast that he found himself at the head of the fleeing group. When he raised his head, a squadron of police officers surrounded him. He shouted his innocence but they wouldn't listen. Immobilized and handcuffed, he was taken to the police station. In the interrogation room, they allowed him to contact one family member or a lawyer. He refused. He maintained he had nothing to do with the burglary that everyone was trying to frame him for. He was firmly denying any wrongdoing. Half an hour went by. Michael's non-guilty pleas were unrelenting.

Annoyed, the police officers summoned the burglary victim to identify the bandit. She was an old lady about sixty years old.

Michael was told to enter the glassed-in room designed for suspect identification. He refused and demanded instead to be face to face with the victim in order to cut short this charade. But the policemen roughly pushed him into the room. The old woman studied the suspect for a few seconds and then shook her head negatively. She was certain Michael was not the right culprit. The officers persisted but she was adamant. "No, he was not the thief. My aggressor was not a man of color," she protested with agitation. "I told you he was a kid of average height with natural blond hair."

The police Chief called the two policemen who had arrested Michael into a room and proceeded to reprimand them. "You know very well that there's a lot of tension in this city already. But it seems you are intentionally trying to make things worse. Two weeks ago, you almost arrested a bank manager for rape under the pretense that he fit the description of the rapist because he was black. One month earlier, two of your colleagues shot at a robber who was black and unarmed. And what did they give as an argument? That the sun blinded them! My God, when will we stop?"

"If you want my opinion, Chief, it's not something we can stop as long as these people keep stealing and selling drugs," said one of the officers sarcastically.

"As far as I know, the big criminals of this world have never been black. Correct me if I'm wrong."

"That's not the point, Chief. These people have a history of their own. It doesn't matter to me whether they're half-breed or not, they all deserve the same fate."

"Listen to me carefully, Sergeant. You're a police officer. And as dictated by your professional code of conduct, you are required to be at the service of the entire community. Don't you ever forget that all citizens are equal before the Law"

"We are the law, Chief," retorted the man in a burst of laughter.

Irritated, the chief threatened, "One more of your stupid remarks and I'll have you demoted to the archives department."

Turning to the other, he continued, "Don't you have anything to say?"

"What can I say? That's life, chief. It's not always fair."

Michael listened, undisturbed. The chief of police left the room, his two hands up in the air in frustration. He invited Michael into the next room, and apologized. Michael accepted his apology with modesty. One of the police officers asked him if he had any particular request. Michael answered yes and explained that he had just arrived into the country a week ago and that he would need a job within the next few days. The officers looked at each other. One of them said he had a friend at the office of municipal services who was currently hiring. He asked Michael to wait. The man left momentarily to the office next door. When he returned, he handed an envelope to Michael. "I will contact him tonight. What you have to do is show up tomorrow morning. He will have something for you. Just don't expect too much. You have to be flexible when you are first starting."

Smiling, Michael took the envelope. He shook hands with everyone and left.

The next day, Michael arrived wearing a three-piece suit. He was expected by the human resource manager. The introduction was cordial and the results were fantastic. Michael was offered the position of parking violation officer in City Hall.

Following a three-month probationary period, Michael was recognized as a permanent employee. His fast integration surprised all the cynics. But Michael didn't let the primitive thinking around him affect him. Certainly many envied him for the position he held but for Michael, his true center of interest was somewhere else. To be a Tae-Kwon Do master had always been his dream. And he would do all he could to achieve his real aspiration.

Every evening with his knapsack on his back, he would join others at a local club and participate in a ritual of physical exercises. Discipline was a golden rule Michael knew well and he enjoyed it whether he was at work, training, or simply socializing with others. He attracted a particular appreciation in his various settings: the club, his workplace and everywhere he went.

The Man and His Destiny

Michael was well aware of his future and he was determined to get there. He really didn't care about those who judged him according to their own standards. He believed in what he wanted and used his position to build a network for his own business. To him, every person is their own wholesome entity who deserves personal attention, and that was the key which he capitalized to get to his goal. No customer left his office without giving him their personal phone number or business card.

On any given day, he certainly did meet many people from all walks of life. Michael felt good and was thankful for that incident with the police. He was aware of the new world he was going to be part of, and he would not let himself be fouled by place and time. Back then, he was perceived differently by his folks, but now he was enduring another type of marginalization. Sometimes, he would ask himself the same question, "What in the world is wrong with people?" Then, he would promptly answer to himself with a smile on his face, "Nothing! Everyone has the right to think whatever they want." He would always remember his Grandma's favorite quote: "Any thought only carries the meanings that the concerning party confers." He was on the mission to report one day to his beloved grandma. That's what mattered to him the most.

A year passed by. Michael kept shaping his road towards his lifelong dream. Although he was at work physically, his mind was not there anymore. A job that requires him to sit all day long didn't fit an athlete of his caliber. Having his own private Tae-Kwon Do School was all he could think about. He could no longer hide it. It was time to move on. Every day, he would count the new business cards he collected, consult his phone book to make sure his mailing list was adding up, and after counting them over and over, he smiled and comforted himself that the time of self-sufficiency was finally at his fingertips.

On his one year anniversary at his job, Michael tidied his office and was getting ready to leave at four o'clock, when a young brunette in her mid-twenties entered. He gestured to let her know that the office was closed, but she simply ignored him. He felt a rage coming on, but held it in. He wanted to throw her out, but didn't have the courage. He stood there, staring at her impatiently, waiting for her to leave. Contrary to his expectations, she smiled at him, introduced herself, "I am Sophie. Nice to meet you, Mikey."

Michael felt a strange sensation. Of all the people in the world, only two… no, three… called him by his nickname: his grandma, Sabine, and his friend Eliane.

Here, everybody called him by his family name, which he didn't appreciate it at first, but managed to get used to it. Now to hear a stranger calling him by that nickname was a big surprise, and quite intriguing.

"Did you call me 'Mikey'?" asked Michael, amused.

"Someone very fond of you spoke to me about you, but I won't say who it is unless you do me a small favor. I know that the office is closing, but I really can't afford another ticket. Someone's been decorating my car with these damned little yellow slips the past three days…in front of my house."

Without saying a word, Michael settled comfortably at his desk and started to fill out some forms. She gave him her driver's license and a piece of paper on which she had scribbled a note. While he was writing, Sophie told him her life story, from her birth to her last heartbreak. She was very excited in telling him how she almost landed a top modeling job. The stint lasted only three days, but she kept a solid memory of it.

Suddenly, she became agitated, "That idiot, because I'm an open-hearted person, he thought I was stupid. He wanted me to pose nude, but I said I would never and I slammed the door behind me."

Michael whispered, "That's good."

Sophie jumped up from her chair, "That's good? You don't see anything wrong with posing nude?"

"No, I meant you did the right thing by leaving."

She cooled down. "You, at least, understand, but there are some jerks out there who think I should have done it. Oh, I certainly like money, but I prefer working to earn it."

Michael asked why she hadn't sought out more serious modeling agencies. She said she had tried but had gained a lot of weight and they all found her a little too heavy for the job. She decided not to torture herself with all that business of dieting; she liked good food and she wouldn't do a thing to change that.

Michael said, "You're not fat at all. You have a very beautiful shape."

Sophie rose up from her seat, turned and turned again several times, asking, "Do you really think I have a beautiful body?"

Michael nodded his head in approval while his eyes stayed on his paperwork.

Sophie replied, "You're not even looking. You just said that to make me feel better." Michael looked at her. "Sophie, you have a splendid body and you are beautiful... The most beautiful I know."

She sat down and said, as if to herself, "It's been a long time since a man's said such nice things to me. You know, life here is not what I had been led to believe it was. It's actually a rather rotten life. I'll travel all my life if I could effort it..."

Michael didn't answer. He handed a sticker over to her. "Just stick it where the parking attendants can easily see it, and you won't get any more tickets while you're parked in front of your house."

She took her driver's license and put it back in her bag, but insisted Michael keep the little slip of paper with her address on it. She thanked him a thousand times, calling him her angel, her jewel and all complimentary words to make another feel appreciated.

"Mikey, do you know any special place where I could go to take beautiful pictures? I love having my picture taken," she asked.

Michael jumped at the occasion. "The Lakeshore is an ideal place."

"Would you like to come with me? Oh, please, say, 'Yes.'" Her voice was soft and imploring. It was difficult for Michael to refuse, even though it was his intention to do so. Sophie pulled him by the arm and he finally agreed. Michael affixed the sticker on the windshield, and they jumped in Sophie's car and disappeared for a ride to a nearby park. With the ice already broken, they instantly became acquainted. Sophie parked her car and asked Michael to close his eyes. When she told him to open them again, she was half-undressed. Only two small pieces of material covered her chest.

"How do I look?"

Michael was rather embarrassed. He swallowed a mouthful of saliva, sighed, and nodded. Sophie dictated the angles and calculated the proper distance from where Michael should take the snapshot. She couldn't have been more excited. She was screaming with joy, jumping at Michael's neck and kissing him incessantly. All barriers were down.

It was Friday evening. The place, known for its attractions, was swarming with people looking for adventure. Sophie yelled for Michael to hurry up. She wanted to see everything and take in every corner of this lively place. Michael and Sophie were giving the impression they were a young couple in love. They looked as though they had known each other forever. Sophie grew tired and requested a coffee break for her amateur photographer and herself. They settled on a terrace and ordered. She selected a Caesar salad and a mineral water. Michael opted for two hot dogs and a soft drink. They ate in silence and resumed their pilgrimage half an hour later.

Sophie dropped Michael off in front of his building at ten o'clock. They exchanged a friendly kiss and parted company. Michael was visibly happy, but waited until he was in his apartment before exploding with joy, rubbing his hands together, jumping up and down and throwing himself on his bed.

Michael and Sophie became inseparable. Two months later, Sophie came over, announcing that she had missed her period. Michael became distraught, grumbled, and knocked his head against the wall. Later, he apologized and said he didn't know why he had acted in such a manner, when she told him it was a joke. She asked him, if he had something against children or if he was afraid of the responsibility.

"No, no and no," he repeated, appealing to Sophie to not pay any more attention to the panic he had displayed earlier. It was a banal incident and it had nothing to do with the love he had for her. *Love?* Michael asked himself. Maybe he felt something for her, but he knew, for sure, children were out of the question, especially if a child was to suffer what he had suffered. Glad she was not serious. He did have those feelings for her, but he had a lot of work to do, before he could have a family of his own. He knew one thing: This woman made him feel good. Was it enough? When he thought of the possible grief relationships can create, he was instinctively on the defensive.

Michael was suffering and he could not deny it. The internal wound was getting worse. It was affecting him and he feared it would be like this for the rest of his life. He wondered if he would ever be healed. He doubted it, and most certainly didn't want to talk about it with anyone. It would be a disgrace to confess to a friend, to admit that he had been an undesired child! No! Anything but that. She would think he's ridiculous. After all, they're his parents. They gave him life and he owed them something even if he did not know how to define it yet. Moreover, his grandparents had always said that a man must be tough and strong.

Whenever he reflected upon these words, he would raise his head and hold it high. No, he must not cry for his fate. Honor must be preserved!

It had been six weeks, since he first met Sophie. One evening, he announced his intention to leave his position at the municipal office to set up his own business, a Tae-Kwon Do school for children. She looked at him, her eyes opened wide, as if he was from another planet.

"Don't worry," Michael said, a little on the defensive side. "I'm not asking for your opinion. I simply want you to know about it."

"In that case, why do you bother to tell me?"

"I don't know. I just want you to know, that's all," he grumbled.

"When are you planning to do this?"

"In two weeks."

"You can always keep your position and work on your business at night, can't you?"

"It's possible, but I'd rather run my business on a full time basis. In any case, I had a discussion with my boss and he told me that if I needed my post back one day, I could always come back." Looking a little bit happier, he added, "The room is ready and all the equipment is in place. I wanted to surprise you."

Sophie pulled him towards her and kissed him on the cheek. Michael felt a little more comforted. "The sign will read, "Michael's School of Tae-Kwon Do!"

"You know, Mikey, I will support you in whatever you decide to do. What's important to me is that you find your happiness in it." Michael drew her closer and kissed her back.

The following weekend, Michael spent all of his time on the telephone. He had decided to call everyone in his address book. In the afternoon, he distributed flyers on the street. At night, he took out his address book again and called everyone with a "call again" annotation next to their names. At the end of the day, he had twenty registrations and ten firm commitments for enrollments.

Opening day was fantastic. All the children were excited by the challenge of the experience. The average student age was nine, with the youngest of five-years-old and the oldest, fifteen. All clad in white with belts, sometimes so large they drug the floor. Parents were seated in the waiting room, watching through the observation window with satisfaction. Michael began his first speech before his pupils. They listened attentively to the master, as he gave his instructions. He spoke of Tae-kwon Do, of his origin, his enrollment in the Asian culture and of the art of defense by excellence for which he was known for. He explained how martial arts could lead the one who practices it to develop self-esteem, confidence, and especially, the respect of others. He insisted particularly on the notion of discipline as a determining factor of good practice for the noble art of Tae-kwon Do. When he finished his speech, everyone applauded. He gave his pupils a few minutes before leading them into their initial pattern exercise. The observing parents were delighted to see their children working so enthusiastically.

Each day saw new members. The club's membership doubled within six months. Michael's reputation traveled all over.

Exactly one year after opening his business, the club headlined the biggest sports magazine in the country. On the cover was Michael's picture with the title 'The Undisputed Master of Tae-Kwon Do.' What an achievement! Michael was so proud and he sent copies to his father and the rest of the family. He waited in vain for a letter of congratulations or encouragement in return. Nothing came. He was used to it and wouldn't let an absent letter discourage him.

Life followed its course. In time, he moved into a spacious apartment in the suburbs, only a few blocks from his mother's house.

The Past Never Dies

At the age of 24, Michael had already enjoyed the glorification wished for by all good athletes, except his Olympic goal. He was an idol with many distinctions, but he kept a cool head about it.

One evening during one of his dynamic training sessions, two men walked in. One, a chubby, middle-aged, Asian man with curly hair, dressed in white from head to toe with a white tie and the second guy seemed to be his alter ego: a Caucasian, in his early fifties, muscular, wearing a red suit with a white tie. They both wore cynical smiles. Michael stopped the class to ask what they needed. The Caucasian man moved forward to shake Michael's hand to introduce himself and his associate. Michael soon familiarized himself with Sam and Cole, two Olympic recruiters.

Their request was clear. "Michael, on behalf of the Olympic committee and as its president and vice-president of recruitment, we've come to ask you to join our team. Our country hasn't won a medal in martial arts for a very long time. This year marks the first time for martial arts as an integral part of the Olympics and we want to put all of the odds on our side. We know that you are the right man to win. All of the information we have on you matches the success our club is commanding in this country right now. You must join the qualifying round!"

Michael listened. Sam concluded his speech on the following terms.

"You don't have to give me an answer now. We still have some time ahead of us... Here's my card. Your country's counting on you." With an expression of pleasure on his face, he shook Michael's hand vigorously then left. Silence hovered in the room following the departure of the visitors. Michael clapped his hands once and everyone immediately resumed their training position with fervor.

Confusion befell Michael over the next few days. Was it the anxiety that preceded all big sporting events or was it simply a matter of doubt? No one could say. Not even Michael. One thing was clear: The internal conflict was reaching an intolerable level. Painstakingly, he kept trying to instill in his students the childhood dignity he never felt.

The following weekend, Michael invited his closest friends for the evening as he regularly enjoyed doing. The group around the table was always the same. On one side were Sophie and Lucy, the eternal accomplices. To their right sat Sheck, whom Michael met while staying at the International Hostel on Church Street, years after they lost trace of each other since high school.

At that time, Sheck's request for asylum was taking too long and that made Sheck very anxious and worried. When they first met, Sheck was as thin as a rake. But since his marriage to Lucy and with Michael's help, he was now able to breathe a certain joy in living. And he was even getting some fat on his cheeks! Alex, a young Portuguese in his mid-thirties, sat next to Sheck. He lived in the same apartment block as Michael. He was already living there when Michael had moved in. Alex's dear and devoted wife Mary sat next to him. Alex, in spite of his engineering degree, took a job as a technician at a toy factory.

"As an immigrant in a developed country, I am destined to a life as a second class citizen; it is the same for all immigrants, with very few exceptions. People have a preconceived idea about us. All they want is to use us for menial work. And that is a reality we can't do anything about. Either you play the game or you go back home," then he added, "Personally, I have a wife and two kids to feed. I really don't have a choice."

Alex and his family hardly seemed to hold a grudge, like most of his immigrant acquaintances. They were a very happy couple, from the outside, and that was enough.

Sitting across the table from Sheck, Michael was admiring his friends as couples. Even though he didn't really envy them, you could see in his eyes that he wanted to be like them. Sheck asked him once, "Michael, you have everything to make you happy in life. Why don't you get married to Sophie?"

He answered with a hint of bitterness in his voice. "Sheck, things aren't really as you see them. Please... I ask you... let's not talk about marriage ever again... if we want to get along." Sheck didn't push it. He knew his friend... when he said, "No." He meant, "No." A brilliant talker, Sheck quickly found another topic so as not to ruin the mood.

That night Michael didn't sit down very much. He moved around, serving his guests. Words here and there would at times interrupt the loud music they had playing. Later the discussion centered on childhood memories.

"If I could, I would turn back time, in a second," said Alex's wife.

"It was the best time of my life. No bills and no rent to pay at the end of the month, no worrying about tomorrow, and most of all, no taxes," added Lucy jokingly.

Everybody laughed except Michael.

Sheck took over. "When I think about how my mother struggled to pay for my schooling, and I, the little bastard, instead of going to school, I'd run away with some of the neighborhood kids to go and pick fruits in the woods. And when it was time for lunch, I would go home, knapsack on my back, like a good school kid, pretending I had gone to school.

Whenever my mother prepared creamy rice, I would throw a tantrum; I would cry, shout, and throw myself on the floor. All the kids adored that dish, but me. My poor mother would beg me to calm down, before rushing off to make macaroni for me, my favorite. My friends eventually gave me the nickname *'Sheck Macaroni'*," he concluded, with a laugh.

"You were so ungrateful. I still remembered those days" Michael added.

"Come on, Michael. You were the luckiest one of all… What are you talking about?

Michael whispered: "If you only knew…"

Sophie took over and addressed Michael, "What about you, Mikey?! You have not shared anything about your childhood, yet. What moment marked you the most?"

Michael instantly turned pale. He slumped in his chair, as if he'd been hit on the head. The long-lost vision of the goodbye at the embassy suddenly came over him, and he became ferociously enraged. He let out a harsh scream, then pulled the tablecloth off the table, and started breaking everything around him. Glasses, plates, dishes - he smashed everything onto the floor and walls. It was total panic. Sophie tried to hold him and calm him down, but he pushed her away. His other guests took cover in one corner of the room.

Michael finally calmed down and returned to his senses. He apologized and asked to be left alone. His friends left in a hurry. The house was a complete mess.

Sophie stayed with him in spite of Lucy's pleas to leave with them. As soon as they were alone, Sophie erupted. "That's it! Let me tell you, Michael. You have a problem, and it's about time you find a solution. As for me, I've had enough. Enough, you hear? I don't know how to be myself anymore, since I've been with you. When I speak to you about having a child, you rant and rave. You yell. You panic! You never try to understand the other person's feelings. You always want to do things on your own, as if I don't exist. You won't accept gifts from a woman because the mere act makes you feel weak. No…Michael wants to prove he is strong…he has to be a champion. My foot! What type of man are you? You are cold, bitter, and you have a heart of stone. You cannot love anyone and you will always be incapable of loving. You're just a little self-centered…"

No! Not again, the words. *'Michael you are this, Michael you're that…'* He'd heard them too many times. Enough is enough. Michael couldn't stand it anymore. He grabbed gently Sophie by the arms, escorted her out of the house and slammed the door shut. The ensuing silence was numbing. He staggered and sat down on the floor. He took his head in his hands, and for the first time, in a long time, the tears started flowing down his cheeks.

He got up and again started throwing and breaking things around him. Suddenly, he stopped, reached for his address book in his knapsack, and began ripping through his stack of business cards. He found what he was looking for. He walked over to the phone, picked it up, and dialed.

"Hello! Mister Cole? This is Michael Deh. I have decided to compete in the qualifying round for the Olympics. You can count on me."

On the other line, he could hear Cole celebrating with joy.

Michael hung up and breathed heavily with rage. He wanted this fight, more than anything else in the world. It was the only way for him to externalize his anger. And as he always had, he would destroy all those who stood in his way. And such is life; we must live the law of the jungle. Only the strong survive. He would prove to everyone that he is a survivor. Finally, he sighed in relief. He had another opportunity to do it all over again, and now he could go to bed and sleep in peace.

Three months was a long time ahead....Enough time to reflect on his anger.

It was very difficult for Michael to relate well with others. However, whenever he found himself at the club, things were almost perfect. There, he felt real and worthy. He would manage to connect with his students with a peaceful mind. Nothing about his program, his teaching methodology or philosophy, was affected. Michael was an exemplary figure and the role model the parents wanted him to be for their children.

Hanging onto a thin line, Michael desperately clung to his life raft to avoid being sucked into the strong whirlpool of his childhood memories. To stay above the fray was not just a self-discipline he reflected upon, but an extension of the same martial arts teaching that made him the man he was. He was trying hard to define a new purpose of living, find and enjoy the pleasures of life, in the midst of the chaos.

After the break-up with Sophie, Sheck invited Michael to a tropical nightclub to get his groove back. It was a small club, but the atmosphere was captivating. Michael was a little reticent at first, but that changed when his eyes met those of a young blonde. She waved at him discreetly and Michael waved back at her. She smiled. He walked over to her and invited her to dance, which she agreed. At the end of the first dance, he asked her to stay for a second dance, then a third, a fourth, and so on, and they spent the rest of the evening together.

By two o'clock in the morning her life was an opened book. He knew her name was Tracy. She was from a rich family and was highly educated. She traveled around the world, always in first class, and she wrote screenplays. Michael was impressed, and her beauty was just the beginning. Tracy was beautiful, tall and alluring, though Michael did find her a little too talkative. In any case, Michael had decided against any serious relationships, so it really didn't matter much whether she was chatty or not.

Michael offered to give her a ride home at the end of the evening. She smiled and showed him the keys to her BMW. They both went on laughing. No more time to waste. Michael and Tracy disappeared into the darkness of the hot summer night. Tracy led the way, while Michael followed in his Volkswagen Jetta. The trip lasted long enough to serve its purpose: mental preparation for what was to ensue. Before she even got the key into the door, they had begun to savor the forbidden fruit. Nothing at that moment could stop the energy that ignited this bizarre and intense fire that consumed these bodies afflicted with carnal passion. Shoes were quickly kicked off, followed by an aggressive casting off of clothes and undergarments. Almost instantly, they were naked. Their heartbeats increased intensely. The breathing patterns were set high. Inaudible whispered words were lost in the clash of the wild, intense rhythmic body talk. The blended scent of perfume, cigarette smoke and alcohol added to the strange atmosphere. Under the guise of forbidden fruit, Michael and Tracy abandoned themselves to the pleasures of the flesh. They spent the entire night together, their bodies like two entangled robes.

The physical pact was sealed. Now, the time had come for the mind to weigh the benefit of the action. Michael wasn't so sure about the aftermath, but Tracy was already convinced she had found the happiness she had been searching for. She busied herself, concocting hasty and precarious plans of a quiet family life. Unfortunately, the flame quickly grew weaker and soon after the long nights of passion, the relationship fell apart.

That evening after work, Tracy had gone over to meet Michael. At the end of his class, after the children had left, she followed him into the dressing room. There, she threw herself into his arms, wrapping her arms around his neck and her leg around his tight body, covering his face with kisses. Michael's face quickly grew sad.

Unable to control the strange feeling overcoming him, he pushed Tracy as far away as he could, yelling, "You're too clingy. You're beginning to invade my personal space. Give me some breathing room, will you? I need my space!"

Taken aback by his reaction, Tracy stopped. Her eyelids fluttered and tears poured. Of all the men she had previously dated, none had ever humiliated her as much as Michael had just done. Infuriated, she collected her shoes and purse, turned around, and left in tears.

Michael quickly regained his composure, but it was too late. He called out for her to come back, but she was already gone. Back in the gym, he hit the training bag so hard, it ripped and the inners scattered. Michael just sat on the floor. For the first time, Michael was angry with himself.

That night, when he got home, he took out a bottle of liquor and poured himself a huge glass, then a second, and a third glass. Michael was visibly upset. He started pacing back and forth. For almost half a hour, he held his hands behind his back, with head lowered and eyes glued to the carpet. He stopped briskly, then ran to his desk to sit. He took out a pen and a pad of writing paper, pulled up a chair, and sat down. The words that quickly flowed between his fingers were explicit and accurate. He stared at the ceiling from time to time, as if to capture some retreating memory. He was meticulous in his quest to remember every single detail. He wanted to let out everything he was holding inside; everything that contributed to his torment. Not one scar would be left out. He had to tell all. His father had to see all of the wounds that he had inflicted on him, all the confusion he had planted in his mind. His father had to face them all. He had allowed too much wrongdoing, without ever helping. It was payback time….Yes, he would demand a settling of the score and now. He would ask for his lost childhood; the one they had deliberately chosen to avert.

Michael screamed, cried, and wiped his tears, then continued his confessions. He was more outspoken than ever regarding his father's lack of affection and unconcerned attitude. This was the basis of his letter. He didn't want to suppress any words. His father has to know. Suddenly, Michael stepped back. He just remembered something: his father was in intensive care undergoing chemotherapy for his leukemia. What a dilemma! Michael held his breath for a moment, and charged forward with his decision. There was no other alternative. Justice must be served. His father had a moral duty to respond to the accusations. *"With his last breath, if he had to,"* whispered an inner voice. Of course not! Absolutely not! Michael didn't wish him dead. All he wanted was an explanation. He was, after all, the only father he had.

Michael filled both sides of four pages. He neatly folded his letter and put it in an envelope, picked up the phone, and called Sheck. They chatted for a few minutes before scheduling an appointment for the following day. Sheck had some shopping to do. It had been eighteen years since the last time Sheck had visited his mother land. It was first thing in mind with his new status and a travel document. Naturally, the entire village must be on high alert awaiting his return. What else could Sheck do, but deserve the welcoming and get a few gifts from abroad.

Michael knew he had to wait and he was very impatient. He couldn't sleep a wink all night. He was extremely preoccupied by his letter. He wanted to see it in his father's hands. He wanted him to read it and tell him whether he was wrong or not. He was counting the hours. Time was dragging on the clock. The night seemed to last forever. Exhausted, Michael finally fell asleep.

He woke up suddenly at two o'clock the next afternoon. His meeting with Sheck was two hours away. He had to hurry and get ready; otherwise, his plan would fail. This letter is his last chance. He couldn't miss this opportunity. *"Should Sheck leave without it? No!"* Michael couldn't think of anybody else who would be able to deliver his letter on time. Now the only thing to do was to rush to meet Sheck. Michael didn't even have time to dress properly. Thank goodness, it was summer, so Michael could choose his favorite way of transportation: the bicycle. He drug it down the stairs and quickly climbed on, pedaling vigorously. Faster! He had to get to his friend's before it was too late. There was a lot of traffic at that time of the day on Yonge Street, but he had to make it there, nonetheless. He couldn't afford to stop, not even for a moment. Michael kept on, pedaling, pedaling, and pedaling steadily.

The Deliverance

What a relief! Michael had finally delivered the darned letter. Now that he knew his words would reach his father without any problem, he could relax and take his time now. He walked for a little while, pushing his bicycle, then rode for a little while before deciding to walk once again. Then he got on his bike and rode some more. He traveled back and forth on foot then back to the bike all the way home. He put his bicycle in the garage, put the chain on, locked it and walked up the stairs.

Inside, he collapsed into his armchair. He stared for a long time at the trophies that were collecting dust in the corner. His hand reached for a golden box. He retrieved a bottle of whisky, poured a glass, changed his mind, went to the refrigerator, opened it, took a bottle of water, drank it in one long shot, and returned to the couch. He straightened up. His mind wandered and he was unable to focus on anything in particular.

Four things ultimately dominated his thoughts: the letter, his mother, his father and love... Yes love! Michael asked himself: What purpose did it serve in life, other than to cause great pain all the time? What was its purpose in his father and mother's case? He didn't know how to answer those questions. Hands on hips, Michael paced around the apartment, stopped, removed one object her, and putting it there. Everything had to be put back in its right place. Some form of order had to be brought into his life. There was no time to waste.

That evening during class, when he got to the school, he seemed a bit strange. Upon entering the room, the students eyed each other with surprised looks. Michael noticed. He shook his head as if returning back from a nightmare, and pulled himself together. No, not here with the children. He could not betray their trust. He didn't want them to know that he was having problems. The person responsible for the program '*Leaders of Tomorrow*' must be invulnerable and strong. In any case, he had never shown any of them that he led a troubled life, and he wasn't about to do it now. Michael very quickly switched his demeanor back to normal and feigned happiness.

The familiar call that always greeted and called his students to attention wiped out any negative notion they might have begun having about Michael. All together, they screamed back to their master and assumed their usual fighting position. Michael was back on track. The session continued as normally as ever until closing time. Parents arrived to pick up their children. They were telling Michael how delighted they were with the effect that he and his art had on their children. As usual, they repeatedly thanked him, shook his hand and congratulated him. The compliments were endless. *"Michael, you're truly a great guy... Michael, the kids owe you. They will reward you and thank you some day; we thank you now..."*

Michael listened half-heartedly. His mind was on something else. The letter, yes the letter! It was his only concern at the moment...apart from worrying about his friend Sheck being on the plane. The thought going through his mind wasn't a healthy one, *"For goodness sake! Why the devil am I thinking about a thing like this? Planes are the safest means of transportation on earth. It would never crash."* Suddenly his mind froze on the possible catastrophes, Michael shook his head, refusing to dig deeper into this painful thought that invaded him. What he wanted was for such tragedies to never take place again, for all the planes to be safe, so that his letter could reach its destiny as planned. Nothing must happen. His letter would land safe and he knew that.

The last student left the room. Michael was completely restless. He couldn't stay still. He hadn't eaten since breakfast that morning. He had to put something in his stomach and quickly. He washed up and rushed out to the nearest restaurant in the neighborhood. There were many patrons enjoying themselves and eating eagerly. The restaurant was buffet style. Michael blended in with the décor and the ambiance with ease.

It was 9 p.m., when he left the restaurant. There was a joyous atmosphere outside, even though it was summertime, the weather was a bit cool. People seemed to be in a hurry, most likely due to summer planning a later than usual arrival. Climatic conditions didn't matter much to Michael. He didn't mind the cool wind sweeping across his face. In fact, he quite liked it! He had no desire to go home. It was late in the evening when he decided to stroll the shores of Lake Ontario. In spite of the cold, a merry crowd had gathered there. He walked for a little while then sat down on a rock. He put his feet in the water but immediately took them out. It was always cold this time of year around the lake but it didn't bother Michael. He sat, quietly, for about an hour, trying not to think about anything. Silence was what he needed.

Michael went home around midnight. He suddenly thought of Sophie. He picked up the phone, but changed his mind. He turned on the TV, minutes later; fell into a long deep sleep where nightmares were non-existent.

The Irishman

Early on the morning of the fifteenth day following Sheck's departure, Michael was awakened by loud knocks at his door. It was the mail carrier. They were the only ones to adopt this abrupt manner of knocking at people's door. Michael took the letter being handed to him. It was a registered letter from his country. The message was short and simple:

Michael,
Urgent! Please come immediately.
Father seriously ill."

Michael felt a sudden sadness because of everything he had written, but the more he thought about it, the more he knew he'd done the right thing. There was no way he could've let his father die without knowing the torment Michael had carried in his heart. The thought of knowing that he had divulged everything to his father in his letter actual gave Michael some relief. Who knows? Maybe they were on the same wavelength. His father had probably read the letter by now and he wanted to discuss it, to have a father and son talk, Michael speculated in his mind. Back home, parents were always trying to find ways to get their kids to return home. For Michael, this was just an ordinary day, like any other.

Michael had been waiting for this moment for a long time, for years. What an immense joy! The most important thing he had to do was to get things moving. Every little moment counted. The phone book! Quickly! He had to act quickly; he needed to contact every travel agency in town and find out which one could offer him a last minute booking. He didn't care how much it would cost. Everything had a price. Sometimes we all have to go the extra mile to get what we really want, his grandmother had always told him.

Michael got his wish almost immediately. He was able to purchase a seat for the very next day. He was so excited about seeing his country again. Not long ago, he had decided he would stay as far away as possible from that damned place, like a soldier who tries to distance himself from old battlegrounds. Satisfied with his plans, Michael took a deep breath. Then, he remembered his students. He picked up the telephone and quickly called each one.

Michael landed at Nkrumah International Airport after hours of flight. The entire family was there. Almost. The expressions on their faces were sad, yet joyous at the same time. His grandmother was particularly happy to see her beloved child again. She gave him a warm embrace, then looked in his eyes and said, "My God! I am so happy you came as quickly as you did. Your father is dying and he's demanding to see you. Please, don't be too hard on him, Mikey."

Michael threw his arms around his grandmother again. Then, following the emotional reunion, Michael hailed four taxicabs and ten minutes later the entourage arrived at the hospital.

Only Michael was admitted into his father's room. His grandmother and the rest of the family had to wait in the lounge.

His father was lying in bed. His wife was by his side. She looked happy to see Michael. She announced to her husband, "Your son is here."

Anam opened his eyes laboriously and smiled at Michael when he saw his face. Then he offered his hand. Michael took it. Father and son were holding hands for the first time. The husband motioned to his wife to leave, which she obliged in silence. The two men held on to each other's hand tightly and for a very long time. Michael pulled up a chair and sat at the head of his father.

His father began to speak with tears in his eyes. "Mike, I received your letter. I have to confess I was deeply touched. I'm asking for your forgiveness for all the suffering that you must have endured because of my silence. But I want you to know that I also have suffered from this situation. You cannot understand. All I'm asking is that you forgive your old father. The past is done and there is not a thing we can do about it. But we can look to the future. Let us build it on a new, solid foundation. Life requires a great strength of character... the one you have managed to embody so beautifully... persevering regardless of the challenges. Staying behind in the past never offered anything good when we try to deal with today. It's a fact of life. Anyone tells you it isn't so is mistaken about his destiny and the purpose of life. Life is the future. And I want to congratulate you for having forged your own future, my son. It's a pity I was not the father I wanted to be. Fortunately, it didn't stop you from reaching the top. Who knows? Perhaps this painful twist of fate was essential to your destiny. No...I'm joking; there is no reason for behaving the way I have and I don't want to use it as an excuse either. I failed in my duty, and I pray the good Lord he will forgive me for my mistakes. Michael, you are my son and I love you. I want you to know that."

They held each other tightly for several minutes. Then the father continued, "I have a secret to confess to you. In my younger days, my friends used to call me the Irishman. Do you know why?"

"No!" answered Michael, smiling and eager to hear the rest of the story."

"You do know that your mother is Irish, don't' you?"

"Yes," nodded Michael.

"And your stepmother, also?"

"Yes," he answered again.

His father smiled and continued. "After we sent you to your grandmother, I vowed I would only marry an Irish woman, like your mother. This way, no one would ever suspect that you were from a different mother, once you came back to live with me. In my mind, I knew I could not respect your grandmother's intent, 'You know her better than I do, my son, never a white woman. Come back and choose your wife among your own kind. She will suit your needs.' Your grandmother always thought she knew what was best for everyone, but I never listened to her. So every time I met someone new, my friends would ask the same question, 'An Irishwoman again?' Eventually, they gave me the nickname of 'Irishman.' That one, your stepmother never knew about. It is a secret between you and me. If my memory serves me right, she was the fifth woman after your mother. It's a pity all those efforts were futile. I also want you to know that having problems with women is something that runs in the family. I never had any luck with them when I was your age. God only knows how many women dream of one day marrying a doctor…"

He paused for a moment before asking Michael, "Tell me, do you have a girlfriend at the moment?"

"No," said Michael.

"I knew it. You really are your father's son."

Michael and his father burst out laughing. A few minutes later, a dry cough seized the old man. Michael tried to help him, but it wouldn't stop. Then he began to experience shortness of breath and the cardiogram became erratic. Michael screamed for help. The nurses came running into the room.

"We need a doctor, we needed a doctor!" Michael shouted nonstop.

One of the nurses kept shaking her head. Michael got the message. It was over. He walked to a corner, sat down, holding his head in his hands. The commotion in the room alerted the rest of the family in the hallway. One after another, the whole family filled the room. Grandma was paralyzed by the emotions, standing bewildered before the body of her son; the one who was supposed to take care of her funeral was gone before her. She cried and lamented as much as her strength could allow her. All around, different sounds of crying were competing.

Michael walked in circles. After a while, he sat down on the floor. His head between his hands, he burst into tears.

The funeral took place a few days later. Michael took a plane back to the place he considered now his homeland. He felt as though the void inside him had finally been filled. He felt he had undergone some type of healing. From what? He was not sure, but he felt good. One thing was certain: A new bond between him and his father seemed to have been born at that moment; the one he had been missing all these years. The sound, the air, the energy, everything sounded different. He was a different man. He was a new man. He was a healed man. He was ready for his journey.

The Champion

Months went by. The date Michael had anticipated for so long finally arrived. In the stands, the crowd chanted for the different competitors trying to fulfill their dreams. Judging by the loud cheers of his name, it was as if it were Michael's birthday. The confirmed Karate Master was more confident than ever. From time to time, he would wave back to his supporters. When the moment came to enter the ring, he glanced one last time to his students sitting in the stands. There he saw something that made him feel as if he was hallucinating. The person he was looking at looked a lot like his stepmother. She was even waving at him. He shook his head, then looked again to prove that it wasn't an illusion. When did she arrive? Why didn't anyone tell him? Right behind, she spotted his stepsister, Laura. She was shouting as loud as she could, "Go Mikey, go! Go Mikey!" while waving her tiny fingers. She had grown a lot, but her fingers were still as small as before. Michael smiled thinking about that. It was a well orchestrated surprise.

The whole family was present. Almost! His grandmother was not there. His stepmother, his two half-sisters, Laura and Jennifer from his father's side was in the middle of the stands. His mother, his other half-brother and his sister from his mother's side were there. And there was Sophie, right between his two mothers. Michael opened his mouth, but Sophie put her finger to her mouth, indicating to Michael that he need not say a word. He understood instantly where Sophie had learned of his nickname. His mind traveled to that day when he had met Sophie for the first time at City Hall, but it was not the right time for a trip down memory lane. Michael realized it was all a set up orchestrated by one of his mothers. He often wondered how

Sophie knew so much about him only people from the mother land did. Apparently, she travelled two or three times to Africa before they met. Michael somehow learned more about Sophie since they got back together. They never spent a day apart, except the last two days. Sophie practically turned down all his invitations. It was kind of odd. Now he understood. She smiled at him as if she knew what he was thinking. She was more beautiful and exotic than ever, Michael was thinking. Overall, Grandma was the only one out of the picture, but Michael knew she was with him in spirit. She had promised him that her heart would be with him everywhere he went, and he believed her. He could even feel her presence right then.

For the very first time, the entire family had come together to see Michael in action. It was the happiest day of his life. Sort of…

Michael took a deep breath and bolted to the middle of the ring, ready for battle. He raised his arms to greet his family and his students. They all chanted together: "Mikey! Mikey! Mikey!"

The competition started and Michael quickly sent his opponents to the carpet, one after another, under the favorable eyes of his family, students and sponsors. The competition got harder as they approached the finals, but Michael was accustomed to tough competitions and he succeeded in staying on top of the game.

After four fights, Michael had made it to the finals. His opponent was a tough Caucasian in his mid-twenties. With his long ponytail, his special circular combat technique, no one was able to stand with him longer than five minutes. His crude fighting style gave him the nickname, 'The Rocket.' When both stood in the ring, you could see the indisputable rage in the eyes of Michael's opponent.

After the ceremonial introduction, as soon as both men saluted each other, The Rocket sent Michael to the mat with a straight kick to the chest. Michael's family stood in shock. The referee rushed towards Michael to see if he was okay, but he was already on his feet. He motioned to the referee to step back. The crowd responded with a mixed reaction.

In a secret room, old men smoked pipes as they bet, a flurry of activities. In the middle of the room, a huge table was set up to take the punters. Sam and Cole wear respectively the effigies of The Rocket and Michael. They proudly collected the change on behalf of their protégé. The wads in front of the Rocket were higher. Sam smiled incredibly as he struggled to handle the crowd rushing towards him. Cole watched, thoughtful but not disturbed. His eyes were riveted on the big screen TV showing Michael and The Rocket, as the fight intensified.

Michael fell a second time after a strong kick to the chest. The Rocket smiled as the referee restrained him in his corner. Michael positioned himself. He remained very still for a moment until the referee resumed the match. The Rocket increased his kicks but Michael blocked and avoided them with dexterity. Suddenly, The Rocket jumped high to finish off Michael in the way of the Samurai. But Michael quickly dodged and answered with a kick to the back of his opponent, sending him flying outside the ring. The crowd cheered. The Rocket got up, contorted with pain, but quickly ran to the ring, ready to fight.

Michael smiled at him. The Rocket rushed furiously forward, Michael stepped aside, unleashed a blow with his tibia on The Rocket's right femur, then another blow on his left forearm. The Rocket was visibly in pain but refused to give up. Michael kept on with the vicious blows left and right. Repeatedly he hit both his opponent's wounded legs and forearms as hard as he could. The Rocket collapsed screaming in pain. The referee rushed in and pulled Michael away. The fight was over. Michael was the undisputed master in self-defense for the next Olympics selection.

Cole rushed into the ring to congratulate his Olympic aspiring hero. In the audience, the applause escalated to a standing ovation.

From her vantage point high up in the stands, Sophie chanted his name repeatedly. She couldn't stop screaming. Unable to wait any longer, she finally decided to go down, jostling spectators here and there until she made her way through to the podium. People cursed her but she didn't care. At the foot of the podium, people had formed two rows on either side allowing her an easy passage. Michael and Sophie looked at each other for a brief moment before running into each other's arms. They were locked in an embrace for what seemed like an eternity. When Michael opened his mouth, she briefly placed a finger on his mouth before kissing him passionately. The students cheered nonstop. His step-mother, close to tears, tossed a little box in his direction. Michael caught it in mid-flight. He opened it and found a lovely, sparkling engagement ring inside. The crowd started to clap hands. Michael stared long at Sophie. Giving in to the request of the crowd, Michael knelt down on one knee and in a voice full of emotion, he proposed. Sophie looked in the direction of his family as they jumped up and down with joy. She looked at Michael, screamed with joy: "Yes! Yes!"

The whole family proceeded to make their way down to join them. Michael and Sophie stood in the middle of the unbound crowd. Emotions were running high. Trying to get to the future bride and groom was no easy feat. When his stepmother finally reached him, she earnestly opened her arms to Michael and the two hugged for the first time. "It feels so good to see you all", Michael whispered to her. "I couldn't miss this moment. God knows how regretful I am for not being there back in the days. Forgive me", let out his step-mother. Michael's journey had come to full circle. He felt it even deeper when his mother and his step-mother decided to confront the past. His step-mother turned to his mother and said. "You were never far from his mind. What happened between you and my late husband affected a lot of people. I was awful to Michael and I am deeply sorry about that. Michael's mother hugged his stepmother and whispered. "I made mistakes with Michael too." They looked at each other and understood each other's turmoil.

Both women hugged each other again. Michael and Sophie stared at them, amazed. Cole ran to Michael and lifted him into the air. The crowd was ecstatic. That very instant was the definition of happiness and nothing else. Powerless under the pressure of so much emotion, he broke down and wept. His mother did her best to comfort him. High up in the stands, stood his long-time friend, Sheck waving at Michael as he shouted at the top of his lungs: "Pancake Boy!"

Michael raised his head, spotted Sheck, and gestured at Sheck as to remind him of the punishment that came when he was called that name in the good old days. Another person in the crowd screamed "Pancake Boy!" He turned around angrily. That name calling started to irritate him. Those two words were the catalyst of the fighter he became. The village boys knew it back then. Not now! Another person just did it behind him. Michael looked back. Another person screamed in a different direction. And so on, until everyone started to scream all around the stadium, "Pancake Boy! Pancake Boy!" Michael looked and just gave up, shook his head, and bursts into laughter as the crowd went wild, chanting, "Pancake Boy! Pancake Boy!"

www.ingramcontent.com/pod-product-compliance
Lightning Source LLC
Chambersburg PA
CBHW071134090426
42736CB00012B/2122